HERE AND THERE

HERE AND THERE

Immigration Through the Eyes of 18 Teenagers

MCKINNON
PRESS

MCKINNON PRESS
2704 Bexley Avenue
Durham, NC 27707
(919) 943-6501

Editor's Note

This anthology was entirely written by teenagers ranging in age from 16 to 18. Their words may appear more polished than the average teenager because they often completed multiple drafts of each submission. The only edits I have made to this book involve punctuation, grammatical errors, and typos. Otherwise, I did not alter the content in any way. On occasion, I have changed the names and identifying information of the students featured in this book, particularly those students who are undocumented. I am incredibly grateful for the thoughtfulness and courage that all of these students brought to this project.

Part 1: Here

Yarely

Honduras

Today I wish I was Superman (even though I'm more of a Wonder Woman fan if I'm being honest). I wish I could fly away somewhere. Anywhere away from my responsibilities and problems. I wish I could tear down the concrete walls, and crush the metal bars enclosing my father with my bare hands. It's times like these – times when I have more stress than I know what to do with – that I miss him the most.

My dad was arrested in early July. As one would assume, it was completely unexpected. The day was just like any other; he had come home around one pm to eat lunch before heading back to work in Cary. As we ate, we talked about a trip to Virginia Beach that we had been planning for that weekend.

Later on that day, at around four p.m., my mother received a phone call. It was from my dad. It only lasted about a minute, but he sounded distressed. A cop had decided to run his license plate while he got off at a hardware store to buy some materials needed at his job. Before I get into what happens next, I think it's important I explain how owning a car works when you're undocumented.

In order to buy or finance a car from a dealer, you need to have a social security number, which an undocumented person obviously doesn't possess. Some places allow you to use your tax ID number, but that's rare. What most people tend to do instead is buy a used car from its owner. Some people have someone they know finance it for them. The problem is getting insurance and license plates.

In order to get insurance, you must have a driver's license, which, depending on the state, usually requires you to have legal documentation. The same goes with license plates. What I've known many people to do is they have a friend or relative (who is legal) place the car under their name, and insurance policy. That was the case with my parents

My mom's car, which my dad happened to be driving, was under her cousin's name. Her cousin's license happened to be expired, which led to the cop going over to question my dad. My dad then explained he was only borrowing the car, before showing the cop his passport, to prove he wasn't lying.

This cop then proceeded to look up my father's name, to find he had missed several court trials, from 1999-2003, for misdemeanors like speeding, driving without a license, etc.

My father, who is 43 years old, is paying for the mistakes he made 20 years ago. He has been gone for three months now. It doesn't seem like much...until you take into consideration that I probably won't see him for another 3-5 years, and that's if I'm lucky. Lucky, as in he only gets deported, rather than sentenced to who knows how many years in prison.

There's a slight chance he could get naturalized, but I highly doubt it. Yes, that's right. I doubt it. Even when everyone is telling me God will work a miracle. That he'll be fine. I can't help but feel my blood boil.

I'm so sick of hearing everyone's encouraging words. Maybe it's because I'm so pessimistic, or maybe it's because I've already accepted what's (most-likely) about to happen. Maybe it's because I hate being told the same thing over and over again, just as much as I hate when people say one thing but then do/say another.

I hear my mom and dad talking on the phone. "God will work a miracle, you'll see," she tells him. I know she's trying to help him be strong. But just this morning, I heard her and my aunt (who is a single mom of one) talking about moving in together. Perhaps it's to save money, perhaps it's so they can keep each other company. They're thinking of working together at construction sites, cleaning and throwing away trash. I could get my license in January and help take the kids to school. Maybe find a better job too.

My dad has told us if he gets deported, he doesn't want to come back. My mom thinks it would be a good idea for him to go to Canada or Spain, after I sponsor him for a green card in three years. I just want him to be safe.

I'm probably overreacting. Maybe there is still a chance he'll be back home, which is why he's been gone so long. Maybe that's why his court dates keep getting pushed back. I tend to overreact a lot.

My mind used to really go to the worst places during the first days he was gone. I kept picturing him getting beat up by the other detainees, or mistreated by the guards. I was even more afraid his mind would go to a dark place and lead him to harm himself. Simultaneously, I was also thankful my dad didn't become another victim of police brutality. At least he's still alive, I thought. I still think that.

My dad is currently at Stewart Detention Center, in some shitty-ass town called Lumpkin in Georgia. I read online that 93.8% of the immigrants there were deported or gave up on their cases and willingly left the country. There are many reports of serious safety issues. My dad told me it's very cold in there, which has heavily affected his asthma. He's also told me the food there is disgusting. One can place money on a detainee's account for them to buy food, but all that's available is ramen, chips, and some sort of powder-mix for 'hot' chocolate.

My dad used to weigh around 165 lbs. He is now 140 lbs. Because of this, he's been having migraines, but due to the lack of medical attention, all he's been told is that he has to eat. They can't even give him a pain killer.

I once saw a news segment of a man who had been let out of prison after spending most of his life there for a crime he didn't commit, just to find out he had stage 4 lung cancer. I hope this isn't the case with my dad. I doubt he'll be held for that long, but I hope his health (mental, physical, etc.) holds up through all of this.

I can't really do anything about my dad's physical health, but whenever I get to talk to him, I do my best to cheer him up. Sometimes I tell him a joke, or some random fact I read online. Other times I tell him about how fat my cat, Thunder, has gotten (this usually gets a small laugh out of him.) He likes hearing about my goals and ambitions, so I try to fill him in on that even though I haven't had much lately.

Even if he's not here we try to fill him in as much as possible, and include him in any big decisions we're making. I'm honestly trying to do my best. We're all trying, not really knowing for how long we'll have to do so, because that's exactly what detainment is; just an ongoing wait.

**

I hate how I seem like such a downer, but I promise I'm not. I'm just very stressed. It's really just because I don't know how to properly deal with my emotions, so I'd much rather just avoid them, which just results in me purposely distracting myself. Part of it is what's going on in my personal life, but most of it is school. There's a lot of school work I'm very behind on. Keep in mind, it's definitely not senioritis, because it's not that I'm unmotivated. I think it's more accurate to say I feel stuck and hopeless.

I want to leave Durham and go to a big city, but I don't want to leave my family, who definitely needs me right now; or my best friends, who I love with every fiber in my soul.

I want to be able to say I earned a full-ride to some nice private school, and get to experience the college-student life my parents have worked so hard to give me, but scholarships are so hard to find, let alone win.

I want to be a filmmaker, and pass all the stories/scenes in my head onto a big screen, but sometimes I can't even properly form them into words.

Even though I feel like I'm not doing much, I wish I could just freeze time, to give myself a break.

A break from my job. A break from helping my mom with all of our current legal issues. A break from school. A break from all of the expectations everyone has of me.

I remember telling myself, at the end of Junior year, that Senior year would be the best time of my life. Now I'm three months into Senior year. It's currently 11:52 PM on a Sunday night. I was on the verge of having a mental break down until I started feeling my 3rd migraine of the day forming. Life's great, seriously.

I want to believe I'm going somewhere, or at least hope I am (like I used to), but life has just thrown so much at me in the past few months that I don't even know if they're signs I should just settle for something more attainable, or that maybe there is something good to come.

They say you have to go through the worst times to get to the best times. Maybe this is one of those situations?

***

Last week, my mom made me go to a psychologist for the first time. Apparently the lawyer said it could really help my dad if we got them to write a note for us, so she took us. I was very nervous about it. I told my friend Sharon about this and she said since it's a stranger it might be easier to talk to them about what's been going on. I guess that made sense, but I still made a note to myself to not say too much. Especially since my business might be read aloud in a courtroom.

It didn't go as bad as I thought it would. But I definitely might have said more than I had too, though. Luckily she (the psychologist) knew how to word it in a way that didn't expose me. She determined I have recurring moderate depression, and symptoms of PTSD. I guess I sort of already knew this, but it felt weird having a professional officially declare it. It almost makes it seem less avoidable.

Now it's only one day away from my dad's court date (November 28th). I leave tomorrow at three AM. I have no idea how to feel. I'm nervous for many reasons.

Apparently the judge might ask me a few questions, so I asked my mom if she could ask the lawyer what these questions will sort of be like. All my mom does is yell at me, saying they don't know.

I'm pretty aware of the fact that he won't know everything the judge is going to ask, but it's not his first rodeo either. All she has to do is make a phone call, but like usual she's making things more complicated than they need to be. Now I'm more frustrated than I am nervous.

On top of being unprepared, I have no idea how I'll react. This could either go one of two ways: I get too emotional from seeing my dad that I can't even concentrate, or I get angry and end up saying something I'm not supposed to.

It also happens to be in a town called Lumpkin. With a name like that, we're bound to encounter some untamed rednecks roaming the wild countryside, ready to hunt for a group of unsuspecting Latinos. All jokes aside, though, I wish some racist would try me. I may be little and quiet but I will not hesitate, and with the way the universe has been treating me, I'm more than ready to snap.

I just want more than anything for all of this to be done. Then I'll finally know if college is still an option for me.

***

I'm disappointed, but not surprised. Lumpkin wasn't as bad as I expected. I was asleep for most of the way there, but when we arrived all I really saw were dirt roads, trees, and really old houses that looked one breeze away from falling apart. Stewart Detention Center was a lot smaller than I imagined. The whole building was a light gray color, surrounded by two gates. The first entrance gate was between two tall, wooden post lights.

You have to press a buzzer before they can let you in, or out. It took several minutes for the guards to open the first gate, and given that it was 40 something degrees outside, this pissed me off even more than I already was. Then came the next gate, but this was one was a lot quicker to get through. Once you get past the gate doors, there's a long cement sidewalk leading to the main building. There's a huge burgundy sign that reads, "Stewart Detention Center," before the sidewalk splits off to the left, leading to the courtroom.

Once you reach that door, there's another buzzer, and a sign that says you can't bring anything except for an ID and keys into the building. This upset my pastor very much (given that he had his testimony written on his tablet), so much that he called the staff stupid, which doesn't sound very serious but in Spanish that word is considered very offensive.

After passing the metal detector and security guards, you're seated in a small white room. It's very simple and plain. There's a clock hanging on the left, and a board with the court's schedule for the day on the wall directly in front of you. On the right side, there's two doors: one leading to a small hallway where the bathrooms are, and one leading who-knows where that can only be opened with some sort of code. Ironically, two women got trapped inside and couldn't get out, which made my little sister and I laugh for a few minutes.

Above the schedule, there's a framed picture of Donald Trump smiling, which I was very tempted to reach up and grab, to smash against the floor several times. For obvious reasons I didn't, but if asked to do so, I wouldn't hesitate. It felt like I was going crazy just from waiting in that lobby for 40 minutes. I can't imagine what it must feel like to be in there for months, or even years.

As I waited, I mentally rehearsed all that I wanted to say in court, until our attorney arrived. Her name was Jennifer, and I learned that she's Argentinian. She's short, and tan, with long honey blonde hair. Her hair was put half up and half down, and she looked like she was in her mid-thirties.

She explained I wouldn't be testifying anymore; it was too risky. The state attorney would put me under a lot of pressure, possibly forcing me to lie for my dad, which is something she wanted to avoid. After that I just listened to her explain what was going on to my pastor, his wife, and sister (from church) Kenia.

Apparently the main crime my dad was going to be tried for was a case of forgery and uttering from 1997. Uttering simply means to use (or attempt to use) a document that's been forged. In the state of North Carolina, this is counted as two separate crimes, but our lawyer was trying to convince the judge that it's only one, since they were both done on the same day.

The judge was not going to be in the room, but on a video chat. He was actually in Virginia, and was known for being very fair.

Fair as in nice, not white. But he was white.

The courtroom was a lot smaller than I imagined it would be. I'm not going to lie, I thought it'd look like the courts I see in shows like Judge Judy, or something like that.

The walls were also white, and there were two wood benches on each side. There was a wooden fence-looking thing separating us from where my dad and the lawyer were.

We weren't allowed to touch him, or even talk to him. The most we could do was smile and wave. He was wearing all orange, including his socks and crocs that the detention center gave him. His eyes went wide as he smiled at us when we walked in. I couldn't decide if this made me even more stressed, or gave me a bit of relief.

On the phone a few weeks before, he had told us about how he had lost a lot of weight due to not eating properly, so I thought he'd look scrawny and much older, but he didn't. He just looked kind of weary.

As the court went on I noticed there was an interpreter there. I've always considered interpreting to be a good career choice for me, but I can't imagine how emotionally draining it must be to work for a court, especially somewhere like this. I'd be miserable, having to come here every day.

I couldn't see the screen that clearly, but the judge's voice echoed throughout the room.

Directly in front of where I sat was the state attorney. She was a black lady who looked like she was in her early 30's. She had nice curly hair but her face looked mean (or maybe it was just the circumstances we were under.) This was supposed to be her sick day. She was supposed to be at home, in bed, not here. Even the judge was surprised to see her and her pile of tissues.

Despite being sick, this woman was very quick. Quick to point out more flaws in my dad's criminal record than I can recall. She didn't skip or miss any beats. Just when I thought there might be a chance of something good happening, there she was. Quite the reality check.

I could feel the lump in my throat growing bigger, my throat drying up the more she spoke.

As my dad testified, I could hear the nervousness in his voice. I could see him fidgeting with his feet, and scratching at the center of his palm (something I do too when I'm upset.) I could feel that lady's intense glare as if it were on me.

Behind me, I could hear my pastor sniffling, crying, and silently praying. I wish I had enough faith to pray; maybe that would've eased the migraine forming in my head.

My dad ended up getting a voluntary deportation. On the one hand, this is good because it won't go on his record that he was deported, but rather that he chose to "willingly" return to Honduras. On the other hand, he won't be able to return to the U.S. legally for another 10 years. I'm not surprised by any of this. This is exactly what I expected.

I miss him and I wish things were different, but at least he's not dead or locked up. My sister and I will be able to visit him every once in a while, but unfortunately my mom can't, because of her legal status. I wish this whole situation could be easier for her too.

At some point the judge mentioned the letter I wrote to him. It went like this:

To whom it may concern,

My name is Yarely Gonzalez, and I am the daughter of Raul Luis Gonzalez Torres. I'm seventeen years old, and currently a senior at CE Jordan High School in Durham, North Carolina. Instead of worrying about where I'll be going once I graduate, I'm worried about where my dad is going. Instead of waiting to receive acceptance letters or scholarships (like I thought I'd be, as I've been working hard for the past 3 years), I'm waiting to know if my dad will be deported or not.

My dad is facing the aftermath of the many bad decisions he made 20 or so years ago. He's not the only one though. Since my father's detainment, both me and my family have been severely impacted. Before his detainment, him and I had both planned on finally buying myself a good video camera. I was so excited to finally be able to film a high quality video of one of the many ideas I had daydreamed about over the past years. I could even submit it to one of my dream schools. Maybe USC, or NYU, or Elon, or all of them, I thought. Now I'm not even sure if I'll be going to college anymore.

As a first-generation American and eldest in my family, I can't help but feel like a failure because of this. My whole life I've been taught that I'd be the one to set a good example. I would be the first to improve, and surpass the standards society has set for people like me, like us. But instead of looking for scholarship applications, I'm looking for a better paying job than my 4:30-10:45 pm shifts as a hostess and packer, which I work 3-4 days a week.

Although I'll be 18 in a month, I'm still just a kid. I shouldn't have to be going through any of this. I've spent the last four years working hard, hoping with every fiber in my being that it'd pay off some day. I have more memories of me staying up late to finish homework then I do of me actually living.

Senior year was supposed to be the best time of my life, but instead everything is falling apart. My physical and mental health is spiraling down. The future I wanted for myself seems like it has ended before it even started. It feels like all my hard work was just a big waste of time, but it's not too late.

Whatever decision you make now will not only determine my father's future, but also my own. I'm not asking you to turn back or stop time. I just want you to have some consideration and sympathy for my family and I. I know my dad is not a bad person, just as much as I know how biased that may sound. My father made many, many mistakes in his youth, but who hasn't? All I ask is that you really think this through. Thank you.

Sincerely, Yarely Gonzalez.

He didn't go in-depth about it, but merely acknowledged it. It's nice to know he actually read it and took it into consideration, even if it wasn't enough.

***

Since my dad's court appearance I've had several people tell me I'm so strong. That's far from the truth. I'm not strong, I'm angry.

I'm angry I have to be the one in this position, when I've done everything I could have done good. When I've done nothing but be the person everyone's wanted me to be. When I've sacrificed so much of myself, and for nothing.

I'm angry the system was clearly not made to benefit people like me and my family. America, land of the free...my ass. You're only free if you're rich, White, and straight. The majority of which I happen to not be.

I'm angry at my dad. I'm angry he couldn't use his head for once, even if it was 21 years ago. I'm angry he decided to not own up to his actions, and for so long. Typical of men. God, sometimes I just hate men so much. I still love my dad (so, so much), and I understand he wasn't in a good place. I understand and am aware of everything he's done for my mom, sister, and I. I understand he was afraid, but I'm still angry. "The devil saw a blessing heading our way and was trying to take it away," people say. The devil this, the devil that. Bullshit. You're just as responsible for your actions.

I'm angry at God. I was scared of admitting this for so long, for fear that it could make things worse, but now I'm beyond pissed. God, I see what you do for others. There are people I know, who do all sorts of bad stuff, much worse than whatever I must have done to deserve this, and they don't have to put up with half of the shit that I've had to deal with, and I'm not just talking about my dad now.

For the past five months, church has begun to feel more and more like an obligation. If I'm being honest, I only go to make my mom happy because I know she's hurting. When I hear my pastor or brothers/sisters preach about having faith, I just feel guilty. I don't know where my faith is anymore, and that makes me sad.

I'm sad because I've lost every part of knowing who I thought I was.

I'm sad because I miss my dad.

I'm sad because the dream I've had since I was seven years old, of going to a nice college in a beautiful, big city won't be happening anytime soon, if it even happens at all.

I'm so angry I want to scream till my lungs give out. I'm so sad I wanna cry till I'm as light as a feather, but I can't, not right now.

I don't have the time or the privacy for it. So I guess it's time to put on my strong face, and start being the head of the household. It feels like the weight of the world, plus 20 years, has fallen on my shoulders. Now I know what my dad must have felt like all this time.

***

It's been very hard for me to write. Not because I don't have anything to say, but because it's been hard for me to admit what's really been going on.

It's been so hard to hear about other's accomplishments without comparing myself to them. Especially right now when almost everyone around me is starting to hear back from colleges. Don't get me wrong, I'm happy for everyone, but I wish I could say the same for myself.

I feel like I've let myself down. My family's caught onto it a lot quicker than I have. I'm easily irritated, and I've been isolating myself more.

My mom and I had an argument over this. She asked me why I haven't continued applying for scholarships, or colleges. I told her it didn't matter anymore, because even if I did get at least one I can't just leave Durham (as much as I'd love to, believe me.) Not to mention the fact that I've missed all of my deadlines.

For some reason she decided to act like I hadn't already told her I was going to apply for a transfer program at Durham Tech for two years. As if she hadn't been okay with this. As if I wasn't okay with it, which is why this whole conversation pissed me off in the first place.

She then proceeded to compare me to other people my age she knew, questioning how come they had been accepted into college and gotten scholarships, and I hadn't.

Oh, I don't know? Maybe because almost everyone wants to play it safe and just be a doctor, or nurse. Maybe because neither of their parents were deported. Maybe because they don't have to worry about helping their mom and sister avoid being homeless. Maybe because they're not in the same position we are in.

To top it all off, she had the nerve to say, "You didn't do what you had to do, because you didn't want to."

I'll admit I have been slacking off and I can't blame anyone for this but myself, but she of all people knows I wanted – want – to be like that. She who watched me stay up, sometimes until four or five in the morning, doing school work, and getting up at six a.m. to go to school. She who would see me staying home and missing out on so many fun opportunities, just for the sake of getting my work done. She who would see me getting up early on Saturday mornings, the only day I had to sleep-in, to do things like volunteer work, ACT/SAT prep, and the SAT test. I did all of this for the past four years; not because I had to but because I wanted to. Because I wanted to make her proud.

I wanted to scream this in her face, but I just walked away.

A few days passed and I thought I was over this. I thought maybe I had begun to accept it, maybe even in an optimistic sort of way.

Boy was I wrong.

As I sat in church, I couldn't help but feel jealous. There was a group of guests, maybe about ten to fourteen people. One of them was a woman, most likely in her twenties. I'm assuming she used to congregate there because our Pastor welcomed her publicly and even asked her to come up to the altar to share some words. She spoke about how her and her friends from Duke University felt very welcomed, and they were happy to be back.

I always imagined myself like that. Coming back home from California, during break, after getting accepted into USC with a full ride. Everyone welcoming *me* back, and getting to see all the new people who had started coming to church.

There was this one time last year when a prophet visited our church.

At the time, I was the photographer for my church. I was standing somewhere pretty far from his sight, looking over the photos I had just taken, when out of nowhere he called me to the altar.

He said something along the lines of the Lord had seen my obedience, and that he was going to reward me with scholarships and the ability to travel the world. At the time this was very shocking, given this man knew absolutely nothing about me.

This instance is something my mom mentions a lot, but if I'm being honest…I could care less now.

Instead, I'll just be watching most of my friends leave. I'll have to stay behind.

Ruben

Mexico

The gymnasium lights illuminated the sweat traveling down my face. My hands nervously shook, and my heart pounded repeatedly. I stood still, afraid of others defining me.

"You're speaking for the Better Angels," the master teacher interrupted. "An organization that seeks to depolarize America by bringing the liberals and conservatives together through sheltered discussions."

I attempted to let out a flow of words, but my throat was screwed shut. I stood silent, looking down at my feet and avoiding eye contact. My eyes and mouth trembled just on the thought of being called on by the teacher. No matter how much I tried to avoid it, I couldn't escape it.

"Remember that everyone here is willing to hear and consider what you have to say."

I wanted to believe that, but I couldn't stop reminiscing over the bad memories. I remember the time where I couldn't grasp the English word "sandwich" to order lunch and being laughed at for accidentally saying "candwick." Or when I was called upon to talk about what I wanted to be when I grow up and couldn't answer because I had absolutely no clue. I felt like these memories were shackled to my feet, and they dragged me everywhere I went.

I'm in a safe environment, I said to myself. My eyes glared at my friends and teachers. They smiled and whispered, *You can do this*. I inhaled a wisp of air and retracted it back out. I spent the whole summer break learning English grammar and words in preparation for this. I promised my mother that I would seek out discomfort. Countless nights I stood up, transcending into a world of words and imagery as my hands grasped the book covers and fingers followed the pages of black ink. The faces of the audience gleamed with smiles, and I felt sheltered.

My tongue unwrapped itself, and words soon flowed out. I felt the power behind the words. The same way I envisioned myself as an Astronaut being blasted into space as a child. I told myself that my stutterings and twistings of words were the same as a spaceship that rumbled: both bound to happen. I saw the audience nodding their heads, a couple snapping their fingers, and the sweat dissipating from my forehead. I realized that my Spanish tongue wasn't a tragedy, nor something to be ashamed of. Instead it was something to be embraced.

When I was younger, I had this mindset that I couldn't achieve something because I wasn't smart enough or good enough, and I was constantly brought down by it. I couldn't explain where it came from. Perhaps it stemmed from seeing my father crumble onto the ground on nights after hours of work in the scorching sun. But instead of finding its origin, I convinced myself that it was my nature; this inadequacy was something I was born with.

This mindset manifested itself at every stage of my life, and it crumbled me, just like it did to my father. In elementary school, I didn't learn my multiplication tables until the 4th grade, when I held a reading comprehension level of a 2nd grader. I believed that passing ESL would be unreachable. I wanted to be like those smart students. But I did nothing about it; I persuaded myself that I was just a less-promising person and student. It was like the flipping of a coin that always landed on one side.

The same thing occurred in middle school, and my self-esteem grew worse. The disparity in my writing level in comparison to another student only expanded more. The vernacular of my peers was much more complex in comparison to mine. I sat at my desk watching the glistening soles of my classmates' illuminating shoes. I speedily sank into admiration and wonderment from the lit up Sketchers. I knew that I wouldn't be able to afford those or even get a chance to wear them. I recognized that my lack of self-confidence was my antagonist, and I felt like a statue that could do nothing but continue watching things unfold even worse.

I can't say that I changed overnight. The people I have met throughout my life helped drill out that mindset from my skull. My teacher, Mr. Holthaus, who mentioned that we study history so that we can avoid committing the same mistakes, encouraged me to pursue my intellectual curiosity. Mr. Albright shared and spread his love for writing to me like the sun dancing across an ocean. My mother's words of encouragement pushed me forward as she fed me with her blessings and awarded me those light-up shoes that I dreamt of. My friends' willingness to help me with my schoolwork allowed me to improve academically and become a better student. Mr. Miller taught me that despite my diffident nature, my life experiences also determine who I am. But it was my father's resilience to rise each morning in conviction to secure a better future for me that allowed me to face my antagonist. And every morning at the break of the sunrise, I remind myself that I am working to secure a better future for my loved ones as well.

"Levántate hijo," someone said as they tapped my back.

I bent my elbows to rub my eyes and looked up at her. An ephemeral moment. The rays of light lit the contours of her face. The dusky circles revolved under her eyes from the repeated nights of work. My mother's frail fingers dug into my back once more as she muttered,"Levántate mi hijo es tiempo para la escuela." *Get up, my son, it's time for school.*

My race has always been a part of my life; it reveals itself in the way I dress every morning, my choice of music, and even the kind of food that I eat. My brown skin has affected every facet of my life. It was the frequent question of why my eyebrows loomed over my eyes, or why my skin resembled dirt. "You brown bug." Those words crumbled me; it reached the point that on some nights in the shower, I aggressively scrubbed my skin in hopes of becoming lighter. I was floundering—like being locked in a closet for a thousand years just to avoid seeing the reflection of my color.

I don't recall many of those days. But I do remember, one day, hearing the door to the shower pushed open, a spectacle of light shining through the opening. Two arms crept in and wrapped themselves around my body, and with a sense of elation and certainty, the words, "*Levántate mi hijo.* Be brown and proud, you are not tragically colored," sang in me. I heard my Spanish heart beating inside.

My brownness was not something to be ashamed of; it was not something that was tragic. But instead, it was something to be embraced.

Color is beautiful—its brownness and all of its mightiness: the tamales and revoltijo de romeritos, La Virgen de Guadalupe, and the Sonoran Desert to the American Dream.

Still my windowless home where I stood in place that sifted through dirt kept my aforementioned differences intact. I remember visiting my aunt's home and hesitantly asking her for some corn tortillas and a small bag of brown beans just to survive for the rest of the week. There were days where I came home from school in my torn-up shoes, and my closet mirrored the barren lands of Mars. I was like a rover searching and praying that coins would fall from the sky. But my mother's optimism and her conviction for securing a better future extended to me like the sun dancing across an ocean.

"Look at me. I struggle but I remain resilient," she says *en español. "Levántate hijo,"* she would add, and despite my food insecurity, her words have always fed me.

My mother offered her *lengua* and support in helping me deal with my past. And that has made me who I am. I came to understand that she grew up in a deserted pueblo; most of the neglected kids ended in the wrong path, but my mother chose to be different. *"Nací para ti."* I was born for you.

My mother reminds me of Zora Neale Hurston. Hurston used her words to extend beauty to blackness, just like my mother did to my brownness, like two externalized figures tackling an internalized one.

As I grew older, life didn't get simpler; I just had more time to understand that I am brown *and* beautiful. I am poor but optimistic. I was a child who didn't know how to savor what it was like to be Spanish, but I am hungry now.

To my mother—your words and resilience have guided me; I was a ship ceaselessly rocking back and forth. Only now—I'm moving forward. Your dancing across decades of struggle will end, the dusky circles under your eyes will fade, and my voice will push up along your frail back spelling out, "*Levántate mamá, ya todo está bien.*" Get up mama, everything is fine now.

Comfort

Liberia

Growing up I never clearly understood what love was or in what ways it was meant to affect someone. I only used it because sometimes it was the right thing to say. Born in an African household, it is really rare to have your parents say they love you on a daily basis. It's not that they didn't love me. I guess they just never said it. African parents are what you'll called the definition of "tough love." I was born and raised in Liberia Monrovia until the age of 10, when I moved to the United States with my Uncle who I called Father. I was raised in a small city called Red Light in Monrovia. Growing up I didn't live in a home with both of my parents. My father died before I knew how to spell my first name. I don't remember a lot about being with my father. I barely remember how he looked. My mother and father split before he passed away.

After a year my uncle took us in. My uncle and his wife played this lottery called DV. It's a lottery that happens once a year. If you get chosen, you go through this process that takes about a year to finish. If you have family in the U.S, the process takes less time. Luckily for us my aunt was already in the United States and she was willing to help with the process. The first time my uncle played the lottery he didn't make it. First they played with his girlfriend who later became his wife, then they played with his nephew who was too old to be their son, but they with him as their son. Next they played with my brother, who was too old too. My aunt, who is also named Comfort, told them to play with me and their daughter, and she was going to sponsor my process. Through that whole process I'd learned that everything happens for a reason. My brother would have gotten chosen since he's so smart. He would have made a great use of the educational opportunity here. But I was chosen. I still don't understand why I of all people got chosen. Even now I still don't know why. It took a year for the process to complete. My uncle and I came to the United States in 2009.

Sixth grade was the beginning of my messed up life. Thankfully no one pushed me in the lockers like my cousin said would happen. I got transferred to a new school in the middle of my sixth grade year. Being the new student it didn't take that long to befriend people. But it also didn't take long to lose them either. That's the thing about me; for some reason I'm more likely to have a lot of friends when I first enter a new environment, but soon after that they would just stop talking to me or they would just stop hanging out with me. I used to think that it was because of my accent, or maybe the fact that I was ugly. But now looking back those girls were probably jealous. Not of my looks obviously, but of my ass. Yes, I said they were jealous of my ass. In middle school I didn't know that I had curves until my eighth grade year, and being the only skinny girl with such a big plump ass didn't sit well with some people. But even with all that, guys still didn't want me and they still don't. I would understand why they didn't like me back then because looking back, middle school was a rough patch.

My accent was thick as hell; I didn't know how to dress for anything. And above all that I was "so African," basically being loud as hell and not even noticing it, and always touching people for no reason.

I still had my African ways. Like I didn't understand why kids in my grade would come to school just to fight other kids. I didn't understand why African-Americans were the only kids in my school fighting all the time. Or why they were so up front about their feelings. Like if they had a problem with someone they would confront them. I have never been up front about anything, especially confronting anyone. So whenever I would see the black kids acting "out of character" I would admire the white kids.

I strive to be them. My parents wanted me to be like them. My uncle would always say "these black kids, they're dangerous, they come to school and cause trouble. Instead of them learning they create problems," but then he would always finish his argument with "you can't blame the children, when all they're seeing is a smoking father and a junky mother, what else do you expect them to do." It's not that I wasn't allowed to have black friends, it's just they can't be "too black."

It wasn't until I got to high school that I realized that white kids didn't confront each other when they had problems because they would rather talk behind their peers' backs and smile to their face because they were into stuff like that. And they are like that about a lot of things. I have white friends, but I feel like with them you always have to laugh about stuff that isn't funny. I'm African, so my sense of humor isn't that low.

But Africans have a problem with African-Americans. Especially the older ones that come to the States in their 30s. They don't know the history; they just go by what they see.

For me it's not that I have a problem with African-Americans, it's just that they are not very accepting about other cultures, or changes.

But in middle school I wanted to be white. As boujee as that sounds, I admired them. But I was more likely to fit in with the black kids than the white kids. I learned that the white kids had a way of making you feel dumb about yourself. They weren't wrong about me, though, because I was and still am dumb. But that's the thing I didn't understand – I mean my dad would tell me all this about how black kids are "not serious" and blah blah blah, but they felt more welcoming.

Most of my close friends in middle school were black. And that's strange to say now because it kind of feels like a white person trying to prove they are not racist because they got one black person in their friend group.

In middle school I was clueless as hell. I didn't know anything about American history or culture. All I thought about was getting a boyfriend. Throughout middle school all I wanted to do was fit in. But I was so damn ugly. I used to wear those high knee Converses, and I really thought I was cool. My accent was still thick as hell. You could barely understand a word I said. But I still thought I was cool, which up to this day I still don't understand. But the most important part of middle school is that I still had my innocence.

My dad would sit home all day and watch the news because that's the only channel he knew how to operate on the remote when me and cousins would go to school, and he would tell us about all the horrible things going on in America and that we should stay away from those "black kids," usually depending on what was on CNN, we would get home and would just hear him saying "…all the children in this country killing people," and then he would look at us and go, "Be careful with these white kids in this country. They will shoot you and nothing will come out of it because their parents will say they have a brain problem. So y'all better be careful with who you're calling you're friends."

Eventually I started getting friends who wanted to hang out over the weekends and have sleepovers. They would ask me to come over or go to the mall and stuff. My uncle's favorite line was, "Don't you have lessons to study?" That basically just means, *Get out of my face and go take your book and study even if you don't have anything to study for.*

This one time, I don't know what made me think it was a good idea to ask my uncle if I could go over to my friend's house for a sleepover. I guess I thought since she was African, it wouldn't be a problem. When I went to go ask my uncle, he was confused at first as to what I was asking. When I asked him if I could go sleepover at this person's house, he responded with, "What do you mean sleepover?" So I started to explain and he goes, "What's wrong with your bed? Why are you trying to go to some other person's house? Stay in this house and take your book and study. You over here talking about sleeeepoverrr."

For that whole year whenever I brought my progress report home and I had a C my uncle would be like, "Instead of you sitting home and studying your lessons, you wanna go to someone's house, and here you are bringing home all these Cs." I didn't even go to that sleepover and there was only one C on my progress report, but the fact that he tried to make it seem like I was failing the whole damn school year makes me laugh to this day.

For the first few years in America, every African parent watches CNN or some other news channel on TV so that whenever you ask them to go over to someone's house, we get to hear, "Why you going to her house? Don't you have to study? You better sit in this house. On the news today some kid got kidnapped and was kept in this guy's basement for years. These people in this country are wicked." I just didn't understand why they would only watch new channels that showed the worst stuff happening in America.

So when I tell you that my middle school years were messed up, it's because I wasn't allowed to go anywhere. And because of that I never found a way to fit in.

But even with my uncle telling me all that, I still manage to fall into the wrong crowd. I had African friends, but they weren't allowed to hang outside of school either because all Africans parents basically bring up their kids the same.

Growing up I was always a slow learner with everything. Still am. I took things in slower than normal kids would, especially kids in America. So I was put in a class with a bunch of kids that already knew most of the things that were being taught, whereas I was at the beginning. When I came to the States I didn't know how to read the word "the." I remember a week after we came to the States, we went to go stay with my aunt and her two children. My little cousin picked up a book with the title *Harry Potter* across the front and handed it to me and asked me to read the title. Let me tell you, I said every word you could think of but the one across the book cover. That's when my aunt got a little scared because she thought I was in school this whole time. But I didn't know anything. So not only did I have to adapt to a new society, but I also had to learn how to read, write, and speak.

It didn't take that long to adapt to the American way of talking, but I still have my accent.

Estephanie

Mexico

If my mother Eladia was asked the question, "What's your favorite thing in the whole, wide world?" she'd answer something like her favorite dish, or her family. But the truth was, Eladia had fallen in love with love. With loving and being loved, with the idea of love; everyone had one true soulmate, everyone was born to love others. Which may be an explanation to every single bad choice she made in her love life.

To start Eladia's story, let's examine her life from the beginning. Eladia grew up in a poor town to even poorer parents. Her father, from up-state, tall, and hazel-eyed, married the poor town's bronzed beauty. A classic love story, passionate and romantic. But things didn't always work out for her parents, and Eladia was forced to look after her mother and siblings. She spent more time doing chores than she did playing outside like a lot of the other kids. But despite it all, Eladia was as happy as she could be. She loved her parents, her pets, and her siblings, even when they refused to let her watch her turn at the TV.

When Eladia was only a preteen in middle school, she turned her attention to the boys in school. She had started reading American romance novels, translated to Spanish, and wanted to experience everything she read. Walking down the market with her mother, she imagined walking alongside a cute boy and sharing a fruit salad or street food. When she held her homemade doll, or her youngest sibling, she imagined it was her own baby, waiting for her husband to get home from work. But all the boys in school were just too *dumb*. They giggled at each other when a female student crouched in her skirt-uniform. Instead, she waited until she entered high school to fish herself a boyfriend. Finally, she found a *perfect* guy. He was tall, handsome, had money, and was overall a great person. Although not the only one, he was one of her more significant boyfriends. He set her expectations to the sky for future boyfriends.

Eladia worked her first job as a daycare "teacher" and felt more mature than her friends were. You could say that is why Eladia's boyfriend was ten years older than her. She was careful and respectful of herself, and she liked the attention he was able to give her. He had a full-time job, but was still able to take her on trips to the local carnival, to the mall in the city, and for ice cream in the market. Eladia was a bit boy-crazy, however, and an attention-seeker, so she didn't always commit to one person.

When Eladia made the choice to move to the United States, she knew it would open up an opportunity to meet new guys, to see new faces and learn new stories. However, over-whelmed by the new environment, Eladia wrongly chose to settle in with the first guy she thought she fell in love with.

Working as a cashier in a small Mexican store, she met many, many guys who she shared a lot of similar experiences with. One guy in particular seemed to drop by a couple times a week. He was a couple years older than her, just the way she liked, and he was from a town in Mexico she knew pretty well.

Their young romance started out like any other; timid, giggly, and thrilling. Eladia was known as bold and brave, so she was the one who made the first move. Soon enough, the two were on endless phone calls. Hours each night. Finally going on their first date, Eladia initially thought it wasn't going to be a very long ride. He was skinny, a couple inches shorter than her, and not so mature for his age. But as they got to know each other, Eladia fell in love with his personality. He was just so funny, so sweet, and his jokes made up for his loss in cleverness points.

After a couple months of dating (around four), Eladia decided to move in with him. She was certain they were ready to live together as a couple. Except he did not even have a home of his own. She was squeezed into a three bedroom apartment he shared with his parents and two siblings. Eladia felt comfortable enough. Her "mother-in-law" was strict and sometimes stuck up, but never treated her too badly. Her father-in-law was a sweet old man who she grew a bond with, stronger than the one with her own father. His siblings were pretty nice as well – the girl, a couple years older than herself, liked to party and meet guys, and the younger boy was a teenager who didn't do much but complain most of the time.

Eladia was pretty much happy the first week of her stay. But after a while, her boyfriend started to show behavior she had never noticed before. He seemed to get angry every time there were dirty dishes in the sink. Even if it was only a bowl and a spoon. Except he didn't say anything to anyone in the house, just Eladia. He'd tell her to stop laying around on her butt when there was stuff to do around the house. At first, he'd say it jokingly, with a light laugh and a kiss on her cheek, but after a while, he yelled it to her without apologizing.

Eladia didn't think much of it at first. She figured he was just stressed, as he worked more than being at home. After a little while, he began to call her out on other things. Things that were a little bit hurtful. Whenever Eladia was at home, in her comfortable clothes, her boyfriend insisted she change into something slightly more "pleasing to the eye." She always had to have her nails painted, both on her hands and her feet. Her hair must always be combed neatly, or slicked back with excessive hair gel if she needed to go out on a hot day. Her clothes, though not very expensive, *had* to flatter her figure. She had to look her best, always.

Eladia loved her boyfriend. Or at sixteen years old, she thought she did. "He's helping me become a better person," she'd explain to herself while dressing in the morning. "He just cares about me. No one can ever talk bad about me if I never *look* bad," she'd tell her reflection while brushing her hair after a shower. She thought she had met the love of her life. She always found a reason to justify his behavior.

For a while, Eladia stayed home a lot of the time. When she applied and got a job at a small restaurant, she was excited to meet new people. Except her boyfriend refused to let her befriend any of the other guys working there. His uncle was a cook; he kept an eye on her constantly and called his nephew if another guy stepped within twelve feet of her. Eladia didn't care much for the ridiculousness of the rule. She didn't want to talk to any other guys. She was already convinced she found the right one. There was one guy, though, who smiled at her every time she walked in. He went out of his way to speak to her. Eladia watched him carefully, but stayed alone most of the time. She didn't have any reason to talk to him more than casual coworker talk.

When Eladia was getting used to taking hours to get ready and committing herself to daily exercise, she learned pretty significant news. She was pregnant. Not only pregnant, but also pregnant with twins. The room spun, her eyes rolled to the back of her head. Her body was going to stretch out and sag in all the wrong places. Eladia's belly sunk when she thought of telling her boyfriend. It had only been about eight months since they met. She still had no idea if he was ready to be a father. A *good* one. She tried to convince herself he would be a great dad. But deep down she knew he wouldn't be. She teared up, imagining a younger version of herself being yelled at for "not doing their makeup right." That's when Eladia realized she hated living with him. She hated not being able to dress however she wanted. Eladia cried for hours into her bed. She had ruined her life all because she wanted someone to buy her a teddy bear with roses.

When Eladia told everyone about her babies, they yelled in excitement. She received gifts from all over. Even people she hardly talked to at work congratulated her with two little pink bags. She loved the attention. Coming closer to her due date, however, Eladia seriously thought about what her future would be like. With two daughters cramped into the apartment, as well. She couldn't gather the strength to see what raising little girls would look like. She much less had the strength to confront her boyfriend about it. She loved him and knew he loved her, too. Especially because she had been watching her weight even while pregnant. Eladia did not have many friends to talk to.

When the cute dishwasher from her job noticed her sulking around, he asked her how she was doing. If she needed anything. She hesitated to talk to him. He was a guy. He couldn't understand. He'd call her stupid for letting that type of guy knock her up. She smiled and said she was fine. He didn't ask her again. Eladia had forgotten all about the uncle she worked with. When she got home, her boyfriend was waiting for her in the living room.

"You think you can go behind my back and think I won't find out?" he asked her.

Her eyes widened and she played over the last few days in her mind. All the dishes were cleaned. Their clothes were washed and folded. Her check was in their bank account.

"What do you mean?"

"Yeah, my uncle told me about all of it. You acting like a whore with that poor dishwasher at your job." He blocked her way into the kitchen. "You think you're the talk of the town, don't you? With your pretty clothes and hair. Well that's *all* me. I invented you. You fat ass. All you want to do now is hang around eating those Cheetos talking about your cravings."

Eladia stumbled on her steps. Her vision blurred from the tears in her eyes. She thought she had kept up with her weight. She tried to walk past him to the bathroom so the shower could muffle her sobs. But instead, he grabbed a knife on the counter and brought it up to her nose. *Too fast.* She felt the drops of blood on her face first, then in her mouth. She touched it lightly with her fingertips and grew horrified at the red on her hand. He didn't even flinch. He began to throw everything he could. Plates, cups, fruit. She dodged everything until she fell to the ground. He grew tired eventually and walked out the door, slamming it behind him. He never apologized. Didn't even offer her a hand. She cried on the floor. For hours. Then she stood up and carried her belongings with her.

Eladia was able to move in with an old friend. She started work at a pizzeria and another job at a factory. She kept the restaurant job as well. She held her tummy whenever she felt sad. She worried about her daughters. Even when she was six months along, her bump wasn't uncomfortably big. But she felt relieved when she felt the powerful kicks. She didn't care there was two sets of feet. She gave birth with her aunt in the room. No one else. Being born a month early, her babies were small and whiny. She hated leaving them, but needed to keep up with the doubled expenses. They were a couple months old when she heard from their father again.

"I am so sorry," he wept at her feet. He had brought two sets of the same dress. Little pink tutus with flower cutouts. "I will never harm you ever again. We deserve a second chance. We deserve to be a family. I promise I will never hurt you or them. I promise you will never, ever need to go through pain again."

Eladia stared into his tearful eyes. She hated him. But she loved her daughters. She loved them enough to suffer every day of the future. To give them a father, a real family. She packed her bags that night. She promised her babies she would never make them suffer like she did. She wanted to give them everything she could. There was love she felt for the first time, too much for her to understand. Eladia had always been a lover. She loved the idea of giving her babies the life she dreamed of. You could say that was why she followed him into his car again, carrying my sister in one arm and me in the other arm. Imagining living with him again, with her heart shattered into pieces.

Kay

Vietnam

Many people I encounter have trouble deciphering my ethnicity. My race is a no brainer, but when it comes to a specific ethnic group, the common guesses are either Filipina or Thai. When they ask where I'm from, I tell them Vietnam. *Oh, you don't look Vietnamese,* they often say. Their confusion is well-founded, because I'm not Viet. What am I, exactly? I am Montagnard—formerly known as the Degar. We're a small tribe in Vietnam that settled there and called it "home." The term Montagnard means "people of the mountain" and comes from the French word *la montagne* which translates to "the mountains."

Growing up, I would introduce myself as Vietnamese to my peers...partly to avoid explaining and going into depth about my ethnic group, and partly because I hadn't yet accepted my own ethnic background. It was as if I was almost ashamed of who I am and where I came from. I would disregard anything that had to do with my ethnicity. For example, my native language. Jarai isn't a well-known language. I thought, "Well, what's the point of continuing to learn and speak my language if it won't be of use to me in the future since English is the dominant language in America?" I was wrong. More and more people from my tribe have become refugees in America. The population of Montagnards since 2008 has doubled, and I regret not practicing my native language because I can easily become a translator for these folks and I'd have my career set for me. Not only was I ashamed that I let go of my language so easily, but I was ashamed in myself. Sad, right? In my household, the kids all spoke English to our parents. At first, my parents didn't like it because they didn't speak much English. Now, they've grown accustomed to it and would speak to my siblings and I in English and Jarai here and there.

When I was four years old, my mother convinced my siblings and I that our dad left for good to cover up the fact that he was running away from government officials to keep us safe. My father was persecuted by Vietnamese government officials because he helped people in refugee camps by bringing them food day and night. He would walk miles and miles to deliver food to the refugees. He didn't have a special vehicle that he delivered them by—it was all by foot. The Viet majority discriminated against my ethnic group because we were a minority culture that settled on land that they did not claim officially; we were referred to as *người Thượng*, Vietnamese for "Highlander."

I was five years old when my mom told my siblings and I that we were going to America to see our dad. I was ecstatic because it had been a full year since I last saw him. A full year without seeing my dad in person felt like an eternity for me.

When I first stepped foot in America on July 21, 2006, I felt like any other foreign folks—out of place. Alienated. I had to adapt to the time zone, and that took me about a week to get used to.

Starting school in America was a whole different journey for me. It was a scary first experience. I started school in the first grade. I was originally supposed to be placed in second grade because I had already done kindergarten and first grade back in Vietnam, but my sponsors thought that it'd be better for me to start off with first grade instead so I could benefit from it in the long run. I remember my first bus ride. I was standing on the corner of a street with my younger sister and one of our sponsors. Our sponsor got permission to go with us on our ride to the school because she wanted to make sure we were okay and made it safely. I stood there with my brown and baby pink Sketchers, jeans, a t-shirt, and my high school musical backpack. I was both excited and nervous. More excited when I got on the bus because it was all *new* to me. When I got to the school, my fears and anxiety overcame me. I looked at my surroundings…a huge building with double doors was in front of me. Kids of different colors walked around me, and all I could hear coming out of their mouths was a foreign language. English. The only words I knew in English were, "Hi, my name is" and "Good morning." My heart was pounding. I didn't know how to ask for help.

Not until recently did I take an interest in learning more about my ethnic group and becoming fluent in my native language—which is Jarai. Because I attended public schools my whole life, I was exposed to so much diversity. Seeing other ethnic groups, I realized that some of them embrace themselves and teach others about their culture because they want their culture to be known. That helped me accept who I am and where I came from, which influenced me to crave more knowledge about the history of my ethnicity. I feel as if I'm letting my culture and heritage die by leaving it in Vietnam and adapting to the "American" way of living, so I want to keep it alive by gaining more knowledge about my ethnic background and teaching my peers about it.

Azusena

El Salvador

My American journey starts here in the U.S. I was born in Chapel Hill, North Carolina in UNC Hospital, which makes me a UNC fan. I now live in Durham with my mother and my younger sister, age ten. I also have an older sister age 21. My family is from El Salvador. I have gone about four times, and each time it's been better. My father lives in Corinto Morazan El Salvador; it's a small town and every single person is so kind. They will greet you even if they do not know you. The land is beautiful and there are not many cars, so many people have to ride horses to get places, and I think that is the best part. I love horseback riding. My father gifted me a horse, and the horse is about the same age as me now, and I'm seventeen years of age.

My mother crossed the Mexico border when she was pregnant with me in her belly. She told me how afraid she was to lose me on way to the U.S. She didn't want me to be born in a poor country with no opportunities to make something out of myself. My mother is the most important person to me; she has always been there for me and she understands about so many things.

My life is very simple. I work in an Argentine restaurant with six other people. I look after my mother who is currently doing her citizenship, and the whole process of her doing her citizenship is hard on her and it's very expensive and she has been having to put other things aside so that she can pay all of the hospital visits, lawyer, paperwork. I have been feeling a bit stressed about her citizenship and if she would get approved for it. My mother is the only person I have here in America who is looking after me. She currently has a work permit, but our current president Donald Trump has taken it away from EL Salvador workers, leaving her only two more years to be in the United States. My older sister is twenty-one, and she is the one helping her to get her citizenship. I'm afraid that she would not get approved and have to leave me. I'm still young and I don't have a high income to look after my younger sister and I. The whole concept of immigrants going back to where they came from makes me very angry. There is no reason why anyone should leave. My mother pays her taxes, she works, she has no criminal record, she is a good person. I need my mother.

In El Salvador many people are poor. The salary that people get there is about two dollars and fifty cents a day. The economy in El Salvador is not good; more than half of the country is made up of MS13 gang members, and they are the world's most dangerous gang. Every single time I have traveled to El Salvador I have had to leave my jewelry and nice shoes and even nice clothing because at the airport there are young children roaming around to see who has money and who doesn't. Based on that they kidnap you so the gang members can get money. Thankfully I have not had that happen to me. The life in El Salvador may not be the easiest but it is beautiful.

In the America that I live there are many issues involving poverty, racism, politics and problems with the environment, police brutality and more. These issues aren't things that we should be witnessing around us. Many things have changed but yet have gone back to the ways things were before, for example racism. Being Latina comes with many stereotypes of drugs, women getting pregnant at a young age and not speaking English, but there isn't any official language in America. I grew up speaking Spanish and I have learned the English language, but I still struggle to speak or pronounce certain words.

The American Dream is the "perfect life," having happiness, the desire for money, food, cars, and everything they want, but everyone's dream is different. I think that we have the ability to make a difference. We have the choice to control our life and what happens to it, but I do not think there is any perfect life without having a little stress or simply having to figure some things for yourself or world problems; life is a bit more complex than you might think.

My America is any place where there is diversity, different people with different backgrounds, and no judgment anywhere. My America is a place where I have a small career for myself, a marriage, kids, and a place to call home, no matter where that it is. But my true America is just simply being happy with myself and everything around me and being healthy. I'm a Latina and I am a proud Latina. It makes up part of who I am and what my family is. My American dream is having the luxury of living my life to the fullest and having the most important person in my life … my mother. Este es mi sueno.

Part II: Coming Here

Rocky

Mexico

Pulling up to an empty parking lot, there are no cars around except a black Cadillac waiting for our arrival. The car we're in pulls up right beside it and my dad grips my hand; he puts his arm around us for he knows where this is going. He gets dragged from the truck we're in and gets hogtied, sack on his head, everything goes black and all I hear is the door shut. My brother beside me reaches in the darkness for my hand. Never having been very emotional towards each other, I feel the sweat building up on his palm, and all I can do is hold my tears back. I'm only six, he's only nine, yet we're both being torn apart from our father in a whole new nation, being taken captive, as I would later come to find out, and we have no one to call for help.

My sisters are back in Mexico, hoping the transition is going well. They don't know that we are being separated from each other and that our father is being sent back to the place where it all started, Mexico. Three hours from that moment, we will be locked in a foreign room in a foreign house with foreign people, all of which are foreign to us. Two weeks from that moment we will be released from that room and allowed to speak to my mom through the phone, the first time in a month that we had finally heard her voice. The last thing I heard her say was "*te amo*."

El Paso, Texas is our next stop. We are given to the next family; it is their turn. Taken to their home, we meet a male in his mid-thirties and his fellow Latino-American wife and daughter, all of whom we will be spending the next three days with. They clothe, bathe, and even take us to get out first American meal, McDonalds. My brother and I are at ease for a moment, but we still want to know where our father is and if we will ever see our home and family again.

For the first six years of my life, my family included my three sisters and my two older brothers. I was the youngest of them all. Life never came easy to us, for we were from one of the poorest villages in Mexico, San Juan. The homes were deteriorating, graffiti filled the walls, and blood tinted the sidewalks. My dad worked in the fields and my mom sold food and pretty much anything she could get her hands on; hard work is all they ever knew. My siblings and I would help in whichever way we could. From a very young age we learned to appreciate everything we had, for more often than not, my parents didn't know where our next meal would come from. Someway, somehow, my mom always made whatever she could from the scraps she was given. Yes, I was six, but that didn't blind me from the struggles I saw on an everyday basis. People were killed every day and night, sometimes right outside my doorstep. As hard as my parents tried, they knew that they couldn't keep us from our reality.

Our home had no roof, so everything that was happening on the outside was heard. Gunshots filled the air at night, and screams that would abruptly stop lingered in my mind for days after. Every day I would lay my back down to sleep but my eyes would be kept open with the banging on our outside door.

They wanted my brother.

Since very early on, the oldest of my brothers, Felix, was involved in the street life, and I was more than aware of this. It never impacted my life, for everyone on our block knew not to mess with him. I never really understood why he was so feared, for he was the one I looked up to and the one that could do no wrong in my eyes; he was my brother.

A few months back, the problems in our neighborhood really started to escalate. I began to constantly see my brothers sneak in from a long night out, only to see them smothered in blood. They would always remind me of the risk they took every time they stepped out or stayed in one place for too long. "Be happy it's not my blood," they'd say. I never really understood what initiated the whole rivalry between the two; all I ever knew was that they didn't like blue, and my brothers and their gang didn't like red.

One night my younger brother Erick got into a really bad altercation with this rival gang. The difference between this altercation and the many others in the past was that it happened right in front of my own eyes. I wasn't scared personally; rather, I was scared for him. Fists were being thrown, bloody blue flags danced around in the dark, and I suddenly heard a loud thud. I realized that it was my brother's people against what finally became clear to me to be the enemy. My brother was getting beaten on and I couldn't stand it. How can someone turn their head when a loved one is hurting?

I ran into our small, two bedroom apartment and ran for my sister-in-law, Vicky. I yelled and begged for her to do something. I couldn't just stand there. I pleaded for them to halt, but they kept going and for the first time ever, I realized that my cries had no value.

My brother did the stupidest thing at that moment: he took a gun out of his pocket, jerked his hand back and pistol whipped the guy who he had brought to his knees. Everything froze for a moment, hands were balled up into fist in midair, shirts were tugged but suddenly released, everyone watched. I noticed his hesitation, whether or not to pull the trigger. Erick – or Smiley as he was known – was just as his nickname portrayed him to be, the one who was always smiling. So for me to see this new side of him, it was almost scary, for I had spent my whole life living and sleeping next to this guy I was coming to find out I never really knew. For a brief moment between him holding the gun as the rival stood at the end of the barrel, I thought that he would actually do it. He would actually take a life. But deep down I knew he wouldn't; he was just doing this to prove a point. No one was going to barge into his territory without consequences.

Christmas was right around the corner and we all knew what this meant: Mama was about to get down in the kitchen. Three weeks left and this is where the fun began. My siblings and I would make crafts to hang up in substitution for the luxuries of ornaments and Christmas trees that only the rich could afford. We made what we could out of what we were given. As Christmas day got closer, I began to constantly see my parents argue on the low, which they nearly never did. Something was wrong. They began to ration the food, the clothes we'd wear, the money they spent, everything. It was no secret that money was running low; we knew the drill, though, for this was not the first time we were put in this position.

During the Christmas party at our home, my mom got pulled aside. I didn't know it then, but that moment would change my life forever. My mom didn't know it either, but the very next morning she would be leaving for the United States.

Who would've thought that I would wake up one morning to see my mom cooking breakfast and head of to school, only to come back to the news that she had left us.

I now know that her decision was made in the heat of the moment and that she saw that moment as her one and only opportunity to finally change her family's life forever. As for my six-year-old self, I didn't interpret it like that. I was shocked that someone could just up and leave from literally one day to the next. Right off the bat, I knew it was because of me. I began to blame myself, for I was convinced that something I had done had now driven her away. Regardless of how much I beat myself up for it, I didn't shed one tear. My brothers had always taught me that tears didn't solve anything, and for once, they were right; my tears wouldn't bring my mom back.

Swimming in the pool, laughter filled the outside as the Texas sun began to set. Pool diving and pool chicken fights, cows who were our pets, surrounding us as they drank from the pool and our temporary family was grilling in the back, all in the middle of a gated ranch. Life was once again good. Our horses were running through the field so gracefully with our pit bulls running right behind them pretending to be one of them; even *they* knew life was good.

The good vibes of the hot Texas day were soon cut short when we saw the gates of the home open up. They opened almost instantly, as if we were expecting them. The laughter abruptly stopped and all eyes fell on the white van pulling up to our yard with JUAREZ PAINTING in big bright red letters on its side. The van door swiveled to the left and men jumped out. Knowing the types of things that constantly occurred in Mexico, I got out of the pool and ran to my guardian. But before I could even reach her as she stood at the front door along with her husband, they greeted them and a man swooped me off my feet and placed his arms around me. Having not seen him in over three months, my dad was not recognizable – as I would come to find out, he had gone through hell and back for that moment right there, to have me and my brother in his arms once again. He held on, yet I didn't know what to think. He put me down and placed one of his hands on mine and the other on my brother, grasping our shoulders as the Spanish I had not heard in so long left his lips loosely. *"Vamos a ir a ver a tu ma!"* he said. We would be leaving to see our mom. For once in a very long time, I didn't have any worries and I didn't have any pain.

As much as I loved living in a huge gated mansion with a ranch, cows and horses to raise, pit bulls as pets, and everything I had always dreamed of, it wasn't home. At least not *my* home. I wanted to leave, I wanted to hear my mom's voice, I wanted to be in her arms as her soft, baby smooth gentle hands caressed my hair. Most of all, I just wanted my mom.

After leaving Texas, the drive to the North was more than what it really was. I became collateral. We spent two days in a little deteriorated home in the middle of nowhere. We were to wait for the others who would take on this journey along with us. Tiny black chickens roamed through our feet, trying to escape us as we followed. The dark would come and sirens filled the midnight air. A trafficking house is where we were. My dad laid us down to sleep, reassuring us that we'd be home with my mother by morning. Of course, that wasn't exactly true.

After leaving the run-down home, we had to walk for two straight days with minimal sleep and minimal food. Fast paced, strong breaths, and sweat dripping off our bodies. Law enforcement right behind us. If any of us were to make a mistake and trip, we would be left behind, for the rest of the group could not risk their future simply because you couldn't watch your step. We entered a darkened forest. Baby clothes, shirts, jackets and half-full bags of food were cluttered all over. I was seven at that time, so the only explanation for all of this was that this is where people went to get killed. The U.S. never seemed so impossible until then.

(Editor's note: Rocky arrived in Durham, NC with her brother and her father after the two day walk, finally reuniting with her mother after more than a year. Her family has lived in Durham ever since.)

Nestor

Mexico

I couldn't believe what I was hearing. I was leaving to go to the United States to see my dad and a better chance to get an education – at least that's what my mom said to me and my sister.

Our journey started by collecting all our money from the bank. We had to spend about $7500 combined with my sister and my mom; it was about $2000 for each one of us. We got the money and we had to find a *coyote*, or a smuggler, to cross us. After we found the coyote he came to our house and explained that we were gonna be in the same bus, but it was important for us not to talk to him so we wouldn't raise suspicion. Then he told us to say we were visiting family in Sasabe in Sonora. My mom bought the bus tickets and we got on the bus at night and rode two days until we got to Sonora. It was alright, but at almost every rest station we got checked by the Mexican military and we lost some central Americans because they didn't have their papers.

I slept most of the trip there. We finally got to this little town, and we had to follow the guy that was taking us to this house, but we couldn't talk to him still because he was kind of undercover, recruiting people to cross. We got on this little run down van. It was about 30 minutes into the desert. We were on this bumpy ass road and we never wear seat belts in Mexico. I don't know why, but even the van's seat belts had been cut off. I never realized that until now. Anyways, I was in the van and it was hot as hell. It was about 100 degrees and we didn't have a working AC. I mean it's freaking Mexico. Sometimes we only had onions with lime to eat. It wasn't good but it kept us from starving.

Anyways, we got to this town called Sasabe, and it had about 30 houses, maybe 40, but no more than that. I was surprised because the house looked run down and it smelled like shit because there were so many stray dogs and other animals like chickens, but the only thing that stood out was the satellite antenna from direct TV. I knew I was not going to be bored. We had to stay in the house most of the time because you never knew if the military would come around to check for coyote hideouts. Only the kids could go out to play for a little bit. I remember I played soccer with the guys in the house; it was fun to get out of the house for a while. That was the first day at that house of the week that we spend there.

The second week they told us they were going to try to cross us in this car, but they didn't tell me I had to share the cut-out back of a small car with two overweight old ladies who didn't really smell like flowers because we could only take a shower every two days. Because of the lack of water I was feeling sick.

The car started to move and I thought at least it won't be long, but the driver got nervous and got out of the car and started to scream, "I can't do it, man! I just can't!"

Some guy screamed in Spanish, "You idiot! Get the hell out of here! You are not getting another job."

We got out, and I was glad because those ladies were stinky. The boss said, "I'm sorry, we are going to take you back to the house."

We got back and I fell asleep right away.

The next day was calm, and he told us that it was too crowded to cross. He told us to relax and to rest. The next morning I got up and I ate my favorite cereal, and all I did was watch TV all day. The boss came, but I can't say his name because, well, you know why. Anyways, he said there is an alternative way, and it's to walk about one night and one day. My mom accepted. It would be cheaper but more work and riskier because there were robbers in the desert who would sometimes rape you if you didn't have money, even if you were a guy, so we took about 100 pesos to give them in case we ran into trouble.

At night time we got on this big van that took us to this dump that smelled bad – I mean it's a garbage dump. We got out and there was this small fence that we went under. I didn't jump. I know you would think I would jump it, but we went under and my mom's friend lost my favorite sweater. We had two guys that were guiding us, one in the back and the other in front. I wasn't even scared. I was scared for my mom and sister; they were out of shape and we were walking for almost a day and a half. I had two gallons of water in both hands. You could only carry two and maybe some in your back, but not too much.

We had been walking for about ten hours when we saw a *mosco*, or a watch helicopter, and it had a big light in the front and the guy said "Hide in the bushes!" The bad thing about bushes in the desert is that they are not bushes, they are just branches with thorns, and I mean big thorns. I ran as fast as I could to these thorn bushes and I slid into them, protecting my face. I got some thorns stuck in my legs, but I protected my face. I was lucky because I was wearing all black clothes. That's what you're supposed to do so it's hard to spot you from above at night.

We waited for about ten minutes until everything was clear. I got up and took the thorns that were in my legs. It hurt, I'm not gonna lie. It was like little Mexicans had stabbed me a few times in my legs. We started walking again, and by this time it was dawn and I was beat and I had on a big jacket. I had to take it off. It was about 99 degrees, and imagine wearing all black cloths.

We kept walking for another five hours, and we got to this place where there was this road and a bunch of black bags, some with water bottles and clothes. We sat down and started to eat tuna from a can with crackers. I was so hungry, but we had to save some just in case as the day went by. The *tuya* told us we were gonna spend the night there. I wasn't very happy because we had to rub garlic all over us to keep animals like snakes and scorpions away. It was the worst.

As we went to sleep it got so damn cold. I wish my mom's friend hadn't lost my favorite sweater. It got to about 10 degrees. We were all on the hard desert ground, only covered by a blanket. I was at the end of the blanket, and my back was freezing. I fell to sleep and I slept okay but not great. I slept in the desert with garlic smell and cold weather.

The next day we got up and the first thing they told us was, they aren't picking us up, so there is a choice: let *la migra* catch us and try again or walk all the way back. My mom's heart dropped. She was pissed and told them she wouldn't risk us anymore, so she said, "Let's get caught." I was sad that my mom gave up. I didn't want to get filed as an illegal.

We looked for extra water because I only had half a gallon left. I looked in the black bags and I found some. It didn't look that clean but it was better than drinking our piss – that's what people do when you run out of water. We were just sitting there and this car stopped and it was two white guys with what looked like officer outfits, and everybody who didn't want to get caught ran so fast, even our guys that were guiding us. We stayed put and even waved at the two whites, but they got back into their truck and left.

We had no choice but to walk back now. I guess it wasn't our destiny to get caught. I was tired, but the extra water I found helped me and my sister – me especially because I had to carry my sister for quite some time. We walked all the way back to Mexico. This time we walked for a full day with no breaks so we could get there faster. We only took a day to get back, but we walked for about 18 hours, and we got back to where we started at the garbage dump. We went under the fence – you could say we unmigrated.

The van picked us up and we got back to the house. I remember I had lost about 10 pounds from starving and walking. They gave us chicken soup to eat. I remember that smell was the best, finally something that had not been cooked out of a can.

This is not the full story, just the desert and crossing part. There is a lot more, but this is enough for now.

(Editor's note: Kevin eventually came to America the following year. His family paid another coyote to get them across the border. They drove this time instead of walking across the desert.)

Keylen

Honduras

Help?

The pungent fumes of sweat and worry had been tickling my sense of smell for the past couple of hours. The bus driver had suddenly disappeared, out of nowhere. His quick break turned into a long time, as I felt the mood of the people surrounding me shift to worry. They seemed to call in desperate prayer to the seemingly missing bus driver. An eternity seemed to have passed on that bus, as my mom tried to put on a strong face for me, but I could feel how preoccupied she was.

***

Flashbacks go on repeat in my mind. Drinking too much soda, even when my mom warned me, and having to ask the bus driver to pull aside to let me pee outside, since the potty in the bus wasn't the best sanitary option. Before asking the bus driver to pull up, my mom had given me a bottle to pee in, but I knew that my pee wouldn't be able to fit in there. I think my mom knew that, but she wouldn't admit it; she was desperate. My mom's face was twisted into worry and anger. This made me feel more guilty than any other lecture – my mom's young face was always twisted into worry all the time she looked at me. As a child, I could never tell if she was worried or upset.

My mom somehow received the bus driver's sympathy. He had been acting nasty most of the time we were in the previously cool bus, but he pulled over. My mom pushed me to pee near the road. No one else was looking, or so she said. Despite my mom's attempts to get me to pee over by the side of the road, I felt like the men in the bus might watch me pee, although I never vocalized my thoughts. Before long we climbed back inside the refreshingly cool bus.

Later on during one of the bus driver's breaks, he bought diapers – from the money my mom provided him with – for me to use. I had to place them on, but I had too much pride to actually use them. I didn't think it would hold anything, and that if I did use it I would feel super uncomfortable. I couldn't be more humiliated.

***

All of a sudden men jumped into the bus men who didn't belong.

Some wore tattoos and I wasn't scared of them, maybe because as a child I didn't really believe there were cruel people in the world; I just thought those existed in the movies. I'm assuming the men had rifles, but I'm not entirely sure of that; my mind has blurred out of places here and there. Sooner than later the bus started moving, but to where I can't remember – nor do I want to remember. They started barking orders at the silent group of passengers on the bus. I don't remember too much of what they said, but I do remember when one of them asked if there were any children on the bus.

Everyone looked in my direction.

He appointed one of his men to escort me and my mother off of the bus and into a room that had a bed and a small refrigerator. All the adults stayed on the bus.

Hours later the women came back all red and puffy eyed from crying. I was drinking a yogurt type of thing called "Lala." I remember going up to the women to ask them why they were sad. They just evaded eye contact with me and started crying all over again. I don't know for how long they kept us in that room, but I do remember talking with one guy. My mom's body language made it seem like she would pounce on this guy if she could. My mom later told me the other women had warned her about me getting too close to him. She would always give me the look of disapproval as I came back smiling at her. I then felt guilty and sad that my mom didn't like my new "friend." He or one of his men, I assume, would come in and refill the refrigerator with yogurt and water and I would always go to the refrigerator to grab some of the yogurt drinks. I remember my new friend gave me 500 pesos, and I was so excited and I ran to my mom to show her. My mom just gave me a light smile and grabbed the money, and I handed it to her so she could save it. Up to this day, I have that bill; I just know that I will never use it.

I didn't even think about what made the other women so restless. Everything seemed okay.

Until the men came in the room.

I don't remember their faces, but the woman clearly reacted. The men who kidnapped us had obviously beaten the men on the bus, and the leader of our voyage was especially beaten. Some women teared up, while others avoided eye contact with the men as they were carefully placing something heavy in front of the room.

I don't tend to talk about this event simply because I just don't remember much of it. Reflecting on this particular part of my voyage to America, I'm not so naive to think that bad people "don't really exist," but it makes me wonder about many more things. Like, what happened to the bus driver? Was he killed or was he part of the band that kidnapped us? Why would a band of drug dealers want to kidnap us? I guess the answer to that last question is a little obvious, yet my brain can't wrap around the idea. Was anyone killed? Were the woman raped? Or were they upset about what the drug dealers did to the men in our voyage? I just don't know.

Lincy

Mexico

In April of 2008, my mom, sister, and I came to the United States. The journey began about a month or two before that when my mom had already left for California. She and her current partner left in order to get settled in and have a space for when my sister and I got there. At this time I was six years old and my sister was nine.

I remember the day in April that my mom went back to Mexico to pick up my sister and I from my grandma's house. One thing that has always stood out to me is that she brought a bucket of Kentucky Fried Chicken. Once we said our farewells to Grandma, we headed to the border to cross with our tourist visa. After entering the U.S., we took an Amtrak train to San Diego, then a plane from there to Sacramento. Our new life had begun once the decision to permanently stay in the U.S. was made.

From the moment we migrated to Sacramento, California, we lived with the relatives of my mom's boyfriend. Like many extended families, no one liked each other very well. There was always drama with those people. Once my mom and her partner were able to become more financially stable, they rented an apartment for the four of us to stay in. As they got hired at better jobs and their salaries increased, we moved to a better apartment, then from that one to a grey house in a very friendly neighborhood.

One of my favorite memories from there is that when we first moved in, the neighbor sent us a box of popsicles as a welcome gift. I was surprised by his kind gesture. Some time passed, and once again we moved to a bigger house. This move actually had a reason, though; my uncle and his wife would be coming to the United States to live with us. They also wanted to follow the American Dream. My mom was the first in her family to migrate and my uncle was the second. From our family, we are the only ones currently in the U.S.

A while after my uncle arrived in California, things began to get hard for my mom due to our undocumented status. Her job was firing people, and it would be hard for her and her boyfriend to find new ones. My aunt, being the "wonderful" person she is, told my mom and her partner that there were many job opportunities here in North Carolina. Having no other choice left, my uncle, his wife and our family moved to Durham, NC in June 2012.

Before my uncle and his family and my sister and I arrived in Durham, we took our final trip to Mexico. I always loved visiting my family in Mexico and catching up from where we would leave off from our previous visit. Like always it was an amazing period of time that undoubtedly had the hardest ending. Every time I visited Mexico, I never wanted to approach the end of the trip. The finale meant saying goodbye, crying, and not knowing when I would come back or if I would. It was this trip that marked the beginning of many years during which I wouldn't visit.

After the trip to Mexico, my sister and I came to Durham, NC, then later my uncle arrived with his family. Moving to Durham was a giant shift for me. The tiniest detail that I noticed the most was the amount of trees that populate Durham. I have always been impacted by the difference in setting between Durham and Sacramento. Once I got over this, I noticed the things that I loved, like the diversity and the acceptance that people in Durham give.

At first, living in Durham was tough. Again, my mom had to live with family, which also ended in conflict, now being with my aunt's relatives. This situation ended with major dislike between my mom and some of my aunt's brothers. The next step was getting our own home, which my mom succeeded in, and she found a very good job. Since that moment, we have moved several times and I have learned to appreciate Durham.

Moving to Durham has impacted me in many ways. I have learned many things and I would like to say that I have matured as a person. In a way, moving to Durham was a blessing. A friend that I made here in Durham helped end the abuse that my sister and I were facing. It's something I hate remembering but a reason that I'll always be grateful for this friend. This situation also helped me view the move differently. I'm a very optimistic person, so I see Durham as a place where I got a new beginning and where I went through an experience that made me stronger as a person and made me become closer to my mom and sister. I also believe that this situation has an impact on how I view the American dream.

To me it was never a big deal; I never thought, "Oh we're going to California to follow the American dream."

To this day, I'm still deciphering what the American dream means to me. However, I do know that it means opportunity, a better life in general compared to the one I would've had in Mexico, but it also comes with suffering. As I live in America day by day, I think about all my family in Mexico who I love and miss. I think about the fact that I didn't get to go to my grandpa's funeral. I go through this in exchange for what we call the "American Dream."

If I had to decide whether it's all worth it, I would probably say yes. I have a very good life here in Durham with my small family, and I know things wouldn't be better if we hadn't migrated to the United States. Yes, in California I lived though some of my worst moments, but here in Durham they ended and I could say it's all thanks to the American Dream. The dream of wanting to achieve more, whether it's financial, academic, etc. This dream built me into a strong, young, independent woman, and I wouldn't change a thing. I'm the kind of person who believes things happen for a reason, but I also don't understand why certain things happen. I do know that coming to America was meant to happen, and I'm glad it did.

Rosa

Mexico

The scenery in front was beyond beautiful. The streets were lined up with vendors, selling everything and anything possible. The smell of the tasty, authentic food filled my nostrils, making me close my eyes instantly. The honks of cars, the conversations people had, and the vibrant colors filled the city with life, giving it its own heartbeat. This was a place I called home. A place I still call home even though I stand nowhere near it. This is my source of inspiration. This is Mexico.

Every individual has a story. For many, their stories consist of happiness and joy. For others, however, it is full of grief and sorrow. Whatever the reason, everyone's background is what makes them *them*. When many think of what an American is, they often say that it is a citizen or native who lives in the United States of America. What they fail to realize is that being legal in the U.S is not the only thing that makes someone an American; there is actually more to it than that.

My mom and dad were both born in Mexico. My mother was born into a decent family, and lived in the city of Monterrey, Nuevo León, while my father was born poor, and grew up in a small town. It wasn't until his family moved to the city that he lived well. My mother was raised Christian her whole life. She attended church every Sunday, and was the top student in her classes. My dad was a drunk whose life took an unexpected turn when his best friend invited him to church. That is where my dear parents met. After being married, they had my older sister. She was born in Mexico. Four years later, on my parents' one month vacation to the U.S, my mom went into labor. I, Joanna Soria, was born in Durham, NC.

When I was one month old, my parents decided to return back. In Mexico, my father climbed the social ladder and owned his own business. He settled our family in a nice neighborhood (at that time it was only my older sister and I). Although foreign to Mexico, I did a lot of growing up there, and it quickly became my favorite place. I fell in love with the culture, the foods, and the loving people.

When I was around four years old, my dad told my family some news. He said that our whole family would be moving to the United States because his business was not looking good, and he wanted a better life for us. At first, we did not believe him. After he showed us proof, that's when everything settled in. We would be moving to a country different from Mexico. That meant new people, new languages, and new experiences were to come. I was excited, but also frightened. I would have to leave my friends, and make new ones. I would have to learn a language I did not know.

I remember stepping off the plane. My family was fortunate enough to get here with a passport, unlike many others who suffer crossing the desert. Everyone here seemed to be different colors, but I mostly saw people with white skin. It was weird at first, because in Mexico mostly everyone had tan skin. That day, my aunt and her husband picked us up from the airport. My aunt had arrived in America five years before us, but her story was upsetting. She had crossed the desert with her husband, two water jugs, and a one year old baby in her arms.

We stayed in my aunt's apartment for one year. My dad struggled to find a job the first month. He started working as a janitor. He would receive little pay, and it was sometimes barely enough to help pay the bills. That is when I knew that everything would not be the same anymore. My dad and mom had sacrificed a lot to be in America, and this was how America was repaying them? I was outraged.

Fortunately, the struggles decreased slightly. My dad found a better job where he was paid extra. We moved into a decent house in Durham. We had more than enough to eat. Everything seemed perfect. The country I had learned to loathe was slowly becoming a part of me. I entered kindergarten in the fall of 2005.

I would laugh inside my head when the teacher would speak her weird language. "This is A. This is B," she would say, going down the list of the 26 letters I had to learn.

"No," I would say, shaking my head. I was used to pronouncing the letters in Spanish, and this teacher here was telling me I had to pronounce them another way? No way.

After a few months, I was able to read and write in English. For me it was scary, but weird how I could speak two different languages. Growing up here has taught me a lot. I became a very open-minded person, and am supportive of the right causes. I can even say that my English is slightly better than my Spanish.

Being an American is to have your own freedom. Everyone is allowed to be who they want, with no restrictions. I am glad to live in a place that has many benefits. My parents and family have struggled a lot, so I hope to one day repay them for what they did for me. I hope to one day impact the world in a positive way.

Trees fill the massive place; however, this place also has a city. Downtown is filled with busy streets, great restaurants, and amazing views. This city comes with bull pride. This city is my home. A place where I gained new experiences. This is Durham, NC.

Part III: Here and There

Bethlehem

Ethiopia

Despite all her children and grandchildren, I feel like more of a mother than she is, sometimes. It's hard to dislike someone who you try to call home, though.

I walk into the dingy, blue, but spacious room that occupies just a few hundred square feet on the fruitiful land that is Debre Tabor, Ethiopia. Close enough to the city where she can buy goods easily when she needs to, but far enough where we don't hear the noises of the growing city. Instead, we hear the noises of babies crying and the guests laughing with a cup of *tela* in their hands if they're my age and *tej* if they're my grandmother's age.

The blue room had walls that were largely empty – but that's because the material the walls are made out of isn't the most conducive to placing decor. Regardless, though, in the corner, she had a photo of my father's college graduation picture, a photo of my parents in our apartment that we lived in when my mother first arrived in America with me, and a picture of my sister and I. A photo that everyone in my family has. The photo shows Elizabeth and I at ages 2 and 4, respectively, in a matching, short velvety red dress with smiles as white and radiant as you could imagine. Everything was perfect in the picture except for the fact that my sister refused to let go of my father's silver flip phone. So that made its way into the picture, too. I could only imagine how long it took Waawi to place those photos in a way that wouldn't make them fall to the ground and shatter. But I guess you can do anything when you want the world to think your house is really a home.

She's good at it, though. Waawi's talent is maintaining outward appearances. She always knew what to serve her guests – in fact, Waawi was known as one of the most gracious hosts in our village. Something that was actually quite a remarkable for someone who wasn't nearly as gracious to her own children and whose obsession with looks and money dictated most of her life - which was nothing short of ironic, considering she was married to a priest (it was an arranged marriage though. I doubt Ababa would've picked her on his own. Or maybe he would have).

Her short stature and heart-melting smile find their way around the blue room asking everyone what they need to be added to their plate of *injera*. At Waawi's house, everyone had their own plate, and full *injera* would be added to their plate every time. We only ate together on the same plate when it was just our immediate family at home. I would feel bad for her a lot of the time. She had quite the expectation to live up to as the wife of the most respected priest in the community, but she lived up to it as well as anyone could. I would see her walk around for hours catering to guests who may just be using her and still keeping a smile on her face. I think I've only witnessed her eat publicly once. A day I distinctly remember because that was the only day I spent time with her and *simultaneously* stopped hating her. Otherwise, Waawi eats in the kitchen once her guests leave.

I don't know how I feel about her. I think regularly about how I feel about her but my mind never settles on an answer. For the longest time, I accepted the fact that I hate her, that she's done terrible things that arguably led to the death of both of my aunts on my father's side, but I'll suppress the thought (that apparently only I carry) so I can function around my extended family. But then Ababa passed away. And I cried for her because I know how her life centered around him – how he was *her* home and the only man she ever truly knew. I also then remembered that she was the mother to *my* Baba, the man I love more than I can truly conceptualize, the one that would give up anything -- and has given up everything -- for my sister and I. I didn't know if I was allowed to hate her. I didn't understand what it meant to hate someone that I called home. I'm reminded of this whenever I go back to visit.

When I walk into the blue room with the grass laid out in perfect proportion on the floor, with the coffee set and *jebena* placed perfectly on the mat by the kitchen, and the newly made covers for the seats, I remember that this *is* my home. I walk into the room that is arranged for my sister and I to sleep in, with the mosquito net that I know she bought with some of her savings, and the *goma* slippers placed strategically on the cold floor by the bed as if she knew exactly where my feet would land when I remove myself from the bed in the morning. I realized then that I have no choice but to accept this as my home. She's moved everything from the room in an effort to give space for us to place our items, but we didn't bring much. With our international flights, each of us gets two free bags to take with us. 8 bags between all of us. Of the eight 50 pound bags, only 2 or 3 are given the task of carrying the items that belong to my parents, sister and I. The rest are dedicated to clothes, shoes, and other items to take back to our family. This being said, she may have moved her stuff out for nothing, but it's her thoughtfulness that resonated with me.

When I walked back into the blue room, I just saw my grandmother crying, holding my father's arms. Telling him how much she's missed him and how happy she is to see him once again. My grandfather, sitting silently but observantly in the corner discreetly wiped away tears with his *gaabi* when he glanced at my father. I sat on the other side of the blue room, trying to catch up with my cousins and absorb the millions of kisses that are given to me, but I can't stop looking at my grandmother and father. She eventually sat on the floor by my father's legs, despite his effort to make her sit on the seat again, and she cried even more. Eventually, she came back up to talk to me and said *Alemworke, Exhabier enante setachouign. Exhabier hulet set lig seteign.* Diamond of the Earth, God gave you and your sister to me. He gave me two daughters again.

My father wanted two girls ever since he thought about having children. Of course, he didn't know that his two sisters would pass just a few years after his arrival in America, but to my grandmother, my father having two daughters was symbolic of a rebirth of the two daughters she lost. Again, something that I don't really know how to feel about. She always makes me feel conflicted.

Someone that I'm never conflicted about, however, is my grandfather. Ababa was a graceful old man with words of wisdom that spilled out of hands like ink on a broken pen. He was not only remarkably intelligent but also an amazing listener. When he and my father would go on long discussions about their respective situations, I couldn't help but eavesdrop when I sat by them. He was a quiet man, but when he made a sound everyone in the house noticed. For some reason, not very many people in the house talked to him. Possibly out of fear that they would be bothering him -- a sentiment I carried as well -- but I knew that my days were numbered every time I visited home, so I made sure to at least try. Hearing him talk about his faith in *his* chair in the blue room removed all my doubts about religion at the time. Watching him recite scripture outside, sitting on a stone while occasionally glancing up to observe his surroundings made me feel like I was engaging in mindfulness meditation just by looking at him. He had a unique gift of making someone feel at home just through one simple interaction with him.

One morning, I accompanied him on his daily commute, by foot, to his church. I don't remember exactly how far it was, but it was far enough to have me wondering how he was able to do this twice every day -- especially at his age. Nevertheless, we got to church and I was able to see first-hand what his service as a priest looks like. Orthodox ceremonies are uniform throughout the churches, yet I felt like walking him do *kidase* was an entirely different experience. It made me feel like church was my home when I never carried that sentiment before.

On our journey back, he seemed clearly unwell. I wasn't sure as to why he wasn't feeling so good, but I made sure to try and help him as best I could. By the time we arrived home, only a few minutes passed until he was sweating, throwing up, and even coughing up blood. I hear all of this from my parents when I leave to go to sleep in the hotel I was staying in. I was up all night, tossing and turning, concerned about Ababa and what was wrong with him.

The next morning I visit him in the hospital. One of my uncles recounts the touching story about how they got him to the ambulance. Since the ambulance couldn't enter the neighborhood due to the poor road conditions, they had to carry him many blocks to the ambulance, all while making sure he was still breathing. And the most notable thing, to me, was my aunt catching the blood that fell from his mouth with her own hands because she didn't want him to worry about soiling his *gaabi*. Needless to say, she's one of my favorite people (for many other reasons, too).

My Ababa was sitting there in bed, in the run down room that I hesitate to call a hospital room. He looked much thinner without his *gaabi* and *netela* wrap, and it was hard for me to look. My father repeatedly suggested that I don't come, but I didn't listen. When I wasn't allowed in the room, I was in the corner of the poorly built waiting room that seemed to be an unfinished construction project at best, and I held my journal tightly against my chest while silently dozing off under the walls with paint chipping so severely that I find pieces of it in my hair when I wake up. These poorly kept, chipping walls felt more like home at the time than the blue walls just a few miles away.

Soon enough, he gets better. He tells my father to not spend too much at the hospital for him because my father will "need the money once he gets much older," and to know that while my grandfather was approaching death he was still worried about my father's future never failed to make my heart grow even more fond of him. He returns home once he gets better, but our time to leave was approaching. When the day came, everyone was crying because we've gotten so attached to each other for the last few weeks. When I said bye to Ababa, I was crying too hard to hear what his last words to me were. *That* was my biggest regret, ever. At the moment, I didn't really understand that it probably was going to be the last time I saw him. At least not until I was already on the bus back to Addis Ababa.

Ababa's passing in 2018 only let the regret manifest itself more and more into my psyche. Seeing my father, instead of Ababa, sit in the corner and discreetly wipe away *his* tears with *his gaabi* is an image I will never forget. But even when I had to witness that, I knew I was still at home because the memory of Ababa that I carried still lived. I realized home was wherever he was. It wasn't dictated by the color or material of the walls, or how guests perceived my home to be. In Ethiopia, my home was Ababa.

Khadidiatou

Guinea

When I think about home,
I think about a concrete lodging place
With windows and doors.
Rooms with made beds and ones you just roll out of.
Unoccupied bathrooms with lights on.
Cereal and bread on top of the fridge,
A cabinet filled with trash bags, forks in the sink.
I think about couches and rugs
Facing a big TV
CNN playing.
I think wifi.
A mom slaving over a stove.
Siblings arguing,
Someone listening to music while showering,
I hear cars zooming by,
Possibly going to their home.
I think about where they're resting their head

Paying their mortgage.
The place they fantasize about returning to
After school
After work.
At least that's how my home looks
That's a home?
I do not know if I am traveling through Durham,
Or is it safe to say this is my home now.
It's hard to consider a place home
When you owe no loyalty to where you land
No respect on where you walk.
They don't think like me
Nor do they have values
Morals
Intentions like me.
They're not like me
Very far from me
But I'm too young to decide.
I just follow my parents
Where they chose to raise us
And so Durham is my home.
In a sense it is where I have stayed the longest,
Where all my memories are most complex and detailed.
This is where my friends are
Where I will graduate.
But my home is also Canada
And Guinea

I was born in Guinea, so in a sense I am always tied there.
I have memories I cannot tell you about and things I can
describe to you in great detail. There are faces I associate with

places and scents and touch. My senses come alive all at once sometimes. It's overwhelming but bittersweet. I can walk into my mom's room and smell the incense that she has burning, and it is as if I've walked through Conakry. It is like I have a direct portal to Guinea. I can wear jewelry that makes me feel like an African princess. Dresses that hug my body and itch my body and make loud noises when I move my body.

That is all home to me.

The performances and drums vibrate and raise goose-bumps on my skin, and this feeling of belonging wraps over my shoulders like a blanket, and I cannot begin to explain what it is like to have a sense of belonging. A group to look at and justify the reasons why you are the way you are. Speaking in the language your tongue first knew. Getting excited when you pronounce everything in the sentence correctly, and finding out you indeed did not betray yourself. Trying to never betray yourself.

Home is my aunt's house in Guinea. I remember walking barefoot on the cold marbled floors and wincing. Grabbing any flip flop I see, bigger than my feet usually. They always had the flag on it. I'd walk around the entrance and walk through the bushes. I'd greet the servants and they'd give me hugs. They weren't treated badly. My aunt allowed them to live with her and eat with us. They were like family to her. They treated me like the little sister they left back home somewhere.

It's hard to think of human beings and their lives before meeting you. What they consider home and what scents and memories they associate with things. Home is a subjective idea.

I find home in anything.

Anyone.

My home was briefly the backseat of a car when my older sister Ramata was learning to drive. The instructor told her the directions to my parents' old schools. I envisioned my parents when they were younger, thinner, holding books to their chests with backpacks on. Running from building to building to make it on time. Walking out with their friends, going to eat at the stands nearby. Being teenagers.

My home was also a caretaker's lodging place. She took care of me when I was little and told everyone I was her sister. I would sleep at her home, wake up, and she had already cooked breakfast for me. She always had movies playing for me. It was a fancy place. They had glass windows and chandeliers. A glass cabinet where kept held china.

My home is also the salon. My mom showing the lady a picture of the style I wanted and sitting in the chair eager to look different than how I came in. Having them all surround me and compliment my hair. Seeing black girls plastered on the walls. Wincing and holding my tears at the feel of a comb through my hair, but there's beauty in that.

This might sound contradictory, but I find beauty in ugly things. Like, how the people of Conakry aren't always nice to Her. They pollute the rich land we walk on. I find beauty in the sanded dirty streets and the crowded roads, and the cursing and the honking. I find home in ugly things. Like the buildings peeling and the corrupt government. I find home in the women scrubbing their clothes on wash boards outside, hanging their clothes on thick strings. I find home in women carrying gallons of water on their heads, and their small waists and the beads they decorate them with. I find home in inconveniences; they don't know what it's like to have things given to them on a silver platter. But they work hard. They make their own platter. It's prettier than silver.

I find home in the humid air. It's ironic that my favorite weather is what my favorite place feels like. All the time. Sunny and bright. It's always hot, but there's always a cool breeze. It always rains at night. So you can always fall asleep to a rainfall.

I find home when the women of my *quartier* hold food stands. It is always outside my aunt's house. I walk there possibly 6 times a day. They always gave me their hot batch of *Aloco*. I find home in the spices and the smell of it. I find home in eating with our hands, on the floor, together. I find home in feeding each other, with our hands, on the floor, together.

I find home in the night. Seeing the electricity finally turned on. I find home in waking up my cousin to go pee outside with me. Because I was scared. And everyone was sleeping. I find home in feeling weird that the bathroom was outside the house. Detached. I find home in watching cartoons at night with my cousin because everyone was asleep and the electricity was finally on. I find home in the silence there is when everyone is asleep. Half dead. In that moment, even if I sleep next to someone. For a minute or maybe just a second, it feels like I am the only one that exists. That my thoughts are the only ones alive. I find home in heavy eyelids and dozing off on accident. I find home in twirling on cold sheets, with the fan blowing against my clothes and the rainfall outside.

I find home in the members of my family. I remember waking up in my sleep, moving around and not knowing who I was sleeping next to. Me being curious, I grabbed their thumb and felt their short nail. I knew my mom had acrylics done for the trip and this person did not. Their skin felt like my grandmother's. I knew it was her. She made my mom, so she's the railway to my home. My *nene cherie* from my dad's side passed the dimples down to me, so I forever resemble her in my mouth. My mom basically lives for me and tries to make all my days the best, and for that she is my home. My dad works hard and worries about my future more than I do. So I can live comfortably in a home. And be happy. And even if in the moment I don't realize it, he's the home I need. The one with CPI and cameras. My brother and my sisters are rooms inside my house. Each one is a reflection of me. My brother Boubacar's room is fun and loud. It's the part of me that's fun and loud. There's bookshelves in there and art. It's because I love words and creating crafts. Ramata's room is neat and organized. In there I study and pray. She's the home in me that makes me want to be better. Amina's room is the most alive one. There I dance and act like a kid. She's the child in me. I find home in every family member. We're all related and have the same ancestors. They're the ones that want more for me than I do.

I find home in my friends. They're the furniture and windows of my home. They match my personality and my mindset. I live in their laughter and in their kindness. I live inside their hugs. I make home out of their generosity and pure hearts. They resemble me in that way. We reflect each other. They're me but better.

I can't possibly forget the home that Canada is.

The memories there don't hold the same weight of the ones in Guinea. It's a different type of home. Security.

My yellow room and stuffed animals are my home. Our basement where I would sleep with Ramata when I had nightmares is my home. The bagged milk is my home. The French and English road sides are now my home. The boots and pink snow suit I would wear beneath my normal clothes are my home. Taking them off with my friends before entering the class is my home. Going to recess and being with my friends is my home. Holding the elevator door for the girl in my class who was in a wheel chair is my home. Her hair behind her hair and her *Merci* is my home. Praying in the basement, but not knowing Arabic yet and so just murmuring what sounded like it is home to me.

Islam is home to me. God is my mansion. He is everything that holds my house up. He is the source of light and running water. He is the reason I can lay in bed and even consider night my home. The Quran and the verses are my home. The praying mat where all my worries and pain wash away. As much as I hate making *wudu*, it is something I will force to be home. It's because of him that I am able to experience all these homes. I am nearly a neighborhood. It is because of Allah that I write. That I love to write. Poetry is the doorbell to my home. It rings and alerts everyone of its arrival. So I make my homes pretty for her. I lay juice and snacks on the table for her. She respects me, so her shoes are on the stand at the door. I can talk with my lips closed and she already knows. She gets to know me more and more. And what comes with me. She accepts me the way I am. She knows all my houses. She's been in them too. She knows my flaws, and when I write with her she knows exactly what I mean. She knows exactly who I write and think about.

It's hard for me to speak on what home is when it's not a set place I can walk into, greet people and offer to help clean. I don't only have one home. I live everywhere. I live with anyone who knows me and loves me.

So maybe what I consider home isn't a concrete lodging place. Maybe it's not a tangible thing. I still live in all of these. They've made a home in me. Just like I've made home in them.

When I think of home in America, I think of a lodging place. I remember being almost devastated changing houses. I had left part of me in each room. Everything had meaning and sentiment. A lot of stuff got lost. Pictures and furniture, so it's almost like we never had it. So they only exist in my memory. When I think of home here, I think about the small apartment we lived in for a year. We moved to America because of my dad, and funny enough he was barely in our home. As much as I hated that little apartment, I remember the exact lay out. There were only three rooms, so my sisters and I shared one huge king sized bed and my brother got his own room. Once you entered the house you were welcomed to the living room. That's where I watched the lips of English actors and actresses move to form words I didn't know. That's where I sat bored and lonely. That's where none of my friends ever sat with me.

When I think of that house a certain feeling overcomes my body. It's not necessarily bad but it's not a good one. I remember sleeping near the window and watching the cars in the parking lot. The red street light and the faint conversations. I remember being lonely. I remember feeling disconnected from everyone. There was a barrier between my tongue.

Imagine not being able to communicate. At least I was going through it with my family though. At least in my lonely way I still had people. I think a lot about how I learned someone's first language. How I lived in someone's hometown, where they know all the backroads and shortcuts. Where it's the only place they can call home. I remember sitting in my "home" and having all our stuff from Canada shipped. I remember bursting into tears when I found a letter my teacher and classmates wrote me. Wishing me all good things. I still have it in my new house right now. I don't look at it as often, but I could never forget their faces even if I tried.

Back to the first apartment. Once you're welcomed by the living room, on your right was the circular beige dining table. We still have it. If you walked further you had the kitchen. Small with wooden cabinets. I hated it. My parents' room was beside it and the wash and dryer unit. Our rooms were on the opposite hallway. A short hallway with two rooms and a bathroom on the right. Basic layout. I went to Frank Porter Gram Elementary. An interesting school, to say the least. I remember speaking with my teacher through Google translate. She had blond hair and a thin headband pushing her hair back. She had mascara stains beneath her eyes and lots of powder over her freckles. She was tall and wide. I can't remember her voice but I know it was annoying. She showed me a lot of prejudice. I could understand it through her language. It happened in mine too. I could read faces and body language; she didn't like me. She made me learn how to say "Can I use the bathroom." So, when I wasn't there I was watching my classmates and guessing what type of people they were. Pretending I knew what they were talking about. I don't know if they felt bad for me, or if I was interesting to them, but eventually I made friends. I'd eat with them at lunch and play with them at recess. I'd talk to them in French and they would answer in English. I don't even know if they knew what I was saying. During every subject my teacher made me move to the back. We learned all subjects with her. I remember during math, I'd raise my hand and she would never pick me. Numbers are numbers in my language too. Watching what she did taught me how to do it. My dad would also teach me the whole lesson at home. I made invisibility my home. I soon learned that even if I was the only one raising my hand, she'd rather say the answer than let me. I wasn't bitter, though, just surprised. Nobody had ever treated me like that before.

I remember when my translator came. We sat at a table outside the class and talked. I realized I wasn't the only French person living here. He had a Quebecois accent like me. I wasn't really a fan of him though. He also had semi long blond hair and a mole near his mouth. His teeth were straight and a faint yellow color. He smelled of cologne and lotion. Sometimes like rain. He was my friend too. I remember when the girls I used to sit with stopped talking to me, and I would ask him to translate the conversations around me. I was nosy like that. He'd listen to me talk about the teacher and how much I hated her. He encouraged me to watch English shows. He taught me some phrases and how to start conversations. He told me to read, so I read. One day I came to school and I didn't find him at our usual spot. I understood our time was done.

I started ESL. I was the only black girl. I remember the teacher's hair color, but that's it. The table was a weird shape. It had a cut out for her rolling chair, and she would sit there.

We had non-moving chairs across from her. We were all around the table. It was at least 6 of us. The lessons became a blur to me. I don't remember how I learned, but I did. I worked a lot at home to make it through. My parents were really persistent and taught me a lot.

I left ESL early and joined the normal classes. That's when I walked in and the sounds made sense. They actually came in my ear and formed words in my brain. I started sitting with them while they learned English. She read books too slowly. I got to understand her through her language. I realized I had a better image of who she was in mine.

I made friends with the girls again. This time we talked in English. I had my first crush here. His name was David. He was deaf but he had a blue cochlear implant and he talked to me sometimes. It was the first time I realized how differently each person was made. I remember riding the bus and talking to this girl about how I can speak French. She asked me how to say chair and I had forgot. That's when I realized how English I had become. I remember finally being picked to answer a question in math and saying turd instead of third. That's when I realized how not English enough I was.

I remember watching 106 N Park with my older sister. That's when I got more familiar with English music. Listening to it again and not pretending to be saying the same thing. I remember hearing about the earthquake in Haiti and my dad leaving to help them. I remember going to my first African Party here, being scared of the Haitian women there. Seeing people drink for the first time and act so weird. I remember it being 3 am and falling asleep on the couch because my parents didn't want to leave. I remember house hunting during the summer. We moved to the house I live in now. I like this house. I still share a room with my little sister, but we have different beds this time. We each have our own side. They look very different, seeing I'm girly and Amina is a bit more neat and tomboy-ish. I started my new school, Hope Valley. That's where I've met some of my life-long friends. I met my best friend Jessica. She has naturally straight, white teeth. She had short curly hair that she pushed back with a colorful headband that usually matched her shirt. She was shorter than me and funny. I remember talking to her on the phone almost every day after school. We got separated after 5th grade graduation. We were actually the cutest. As much as that school is a blur, I still get flooded with snippets. I guess I remember a lot more than I think.

I started middle school. I made friends I'll never forget. Wherever life takes us. My first guy friend, Jeyson. He reminds me a lot of myself. He makes me laugh more than anyone. We're still friends. I met my friend Rae Anna, who's just like him. We have the same goofy personality. I met Carmen, who is almost as selfless as me. Wgoud, who was my first Muslim friend here. She relates to me a lot and we have deep conversations about God and she tells me about prophets and jins. Jahlilya, who just inspires me to be a woke and unapologetic black girl. They all gave me a voice and room to explore myself. Jatzyri especially. She changed my life, honestly. She's the reason I have a lot of the interests I have. She inspired me to start my first poem. I remember writing creative writing pieces with her at midnight. She morphed me. She helped me gain confidence, and believe in myself. She helped me be extroverted again. She reminds me to do my homework and apply for colleges and scholarships. I learn from all my friends. They genuinely live in my heart. They're the angels on my shoulders and my best qualities. I don't love one more than the other. They all contribute to the American version of me. Because now I guess I am American. It baffles me how I've lived here longer than I've live anywhere else. I speak English the best out of all my languages. It's scary to think I am changing. That I won't be a parent like my parents.

My music tastes changed, and I started exploring more about different people and genres. I listened to everything from jazz, to electronic, to hip hop, to R&B, to alternative, to afro beat, to reggae. I have memories of me and Jatzyri listening to music, each of us with one headphone. On the bleachers, avoiding the laps we had to run in gym. I remember going to the movie theaters and crying with my friends and sometimes my family. I reunited with Jessica. It was awkward after 4 years but so sweet. Now we see each other every other month. But we talk all day long. She's my best friend.

High school was so different. I outgrew people and thought something was wrong with me. I shed layers of skin, and some of the friends I thought were going to last were the first to slip off my body. I stepped foot into what it was to get to know me. I started to understand what my mom's proverbs meant. All the lessons she always tried to get me to adopt. I started seeing her as an actual human who wouldn't last forever. I felt my innocence was taken my junior year. Not the one you think, but worse. I stopped having a childish mind, and a lot of things that hid behind clouds gave out. I was shown all the ugliness of the world and all the ugly people. Everything became more real and raw. Misfortune happened and sadness was a thing now.

I don't know how to explain having feet in different countries. I have but two feet. My left is here and my right is in Guinea and maybe I have my hands stretched to Canada, but I can't call one of them home and not the other. Each country gets a different part of me. They've all developed different parts of me.

I am from Alimou Mamadou Barry and Issatou Balde
I am from wall corners
Beautiful
Silently
Thiouray
I am from hibiscus
I am from deep conversations
I am from deeper smiles
I am from Nene Cherie and Nene Mamman
I am from aggressive tones
I am from selflessness
From the princess of Dalaba and *ta fenu*. Don't Lie
I am from ripped up Quarans and prayer mats
I am from Guinea Conakry
Yamaku
Tea
From the long mountain walks to wells and schools,
So I can't complain about my AP class
The abandonment of loved ones
Fireplace
Where all pictures and achievements stay
Magnets on fridges can't hold that.
As much as I am ashamed, I'm from Durham.
She raised me.
I got over my fear of roller coasters here,
I went natural here,
I had my first kiss here,

I learned how to drive here,

I lost friends here,

I was naive here,

I went in photo booths and took pictures for the first time,

I held birthday dinners for my 14th

And 15th

And 16th birthday,

I did things on the Durham bull roofs,

With friends,

At night,

Here.

I prayed correctly for the first time

I grew breasts

I made bad decisions here,

I made good decisions here,

I laughed here,

I cried here,

I went through depression here,

I felt defeated here,

I smiled here,

I complained here,

I screamed here,

I stayed mute here,

I grew here,

I changed here

But it's because I love it here.

Zarah

Honduras and El Salvador

My story begins in the 1920's in a small frontier between two neighboring countries. A rocky river divides these two countries apart. Willow and Laurel trees decorate the river's borders. The body of the river itself was intentionally left unclaimed by the countries. Wildlife surrounds the river. On one side there was a cane milling site where there were not many inhabitants. It was a side that still had a lot of its vegetation. The other side was a complete contrast; it was a location where many people lived. Their economy was dedicated to agriculture, raising livestock, and harvesting coffee beans.

In the cane milling site there was a semi-attractive young man, Rafael, who was what people labeled as *Indio*, a term used for those who looked indigenous. Such people tended to be looked down upon by society. His eyes had been set on a young woman with dirty blonde hair and blue eyes who lived in the prosperous side of the frontier. Rafael soon learned that her name was Rosa. Rafael had one characteristic that made him be set apart from the rest: every boy around her admired her from a distance, but he was bold and persistent to try to become Rosa's boyfriend. She refused due to her parents because they stood against his racial appearance and his nationality. But he eventually got through Rosa.

It is a story straight from a cheesy Romeo and Juliet-like movie. They run away together to try and live a happily ever after in a land far from what they have known their whole lives. By running away, tensions between their families increased. Rosa's family announced that they would give a reward to anyone who had any information on where the couple had decided to settle on. They called Rafael a thief, which did not sit well with his family.

Rafael and Rosa crossed a country with no particular directions to follow. They met a man called *Chemita* who let them borrow land to build a house. They lived in poor circumstances, but they managed to create a home for their kids. The family harvested vegetables such as corn, beans, and *yuca*. As one can imagine, having kids places a strain on living circumstances. They were not alone; everyone else was also struggling as well. Work became scarce and eventually solutions became radical.

A little back story on Rafael: he was poor. He made a living off of working at the factory when he met Rosa. Whereas Rosa herself lived a decent life. She may have not had it all, but food was never something that she had to concern herself over. There was always food in the house; however, things changed when Rosa decided to run away with Rafael. By running away, she stepped away from the comfort she never quite understood she had until it was gone. As the years went by, Rosa became less determined, less confident telling her children that tomorrow will be a day of better feeding, and less assuring of the promise of tomorrow whilst kissing her children goodnight. She could no longer bear living in extreme poverty; it broke her to see her children going to sleep with empty stomachs, something she had never experienced herself as a child.

Then it was decided that they would all take a trip to Rosa's hometown and visit her parents. Her parents held a big dinner as a celebration of their daughter's return. The children were happy to fill their mouths with a lot of food. They had previously never witnessed as much food as they did on the dinner table that evening. The children were completely oblivious as to the real reason why they were at their grandparents. They did not know that it would be their last time eating together as a family.

The next day came and the kids were struggling to keep up with their parents. The train was going to arrive any minute. Just picture it, the sun is rising and the fruitful land has a golden hue. The rooster's cries sounded like old news as the family hurries to the station. Rafael and Rosa are in the middle of a circle that their kids naturally formed. They stand looking at each other. Rosa starts crying. To the children's knowledge, their father has to go home but will be right back. They do not understand what the big deal is all about.

All the family has gathered around the improvised train station. The sky was welcoming the sun's golden rays.

"I want to go with dad!" the words come slipping out of the eldest son's mouth. He sees his mother's hurt eyes.

"Sweetie, stay with me here. Father will arrive back soon." Rosa glances at Rafael, slightly nodding her head.

"Son, listen to your mother." Rafael bends down at my eye level.

"But I want to eat all the food my mom made that is at home." The boy was stubborn even at a young age. His dad glances at his mother and all the children.

"Fine, since I'll be back soon you can come with me." Rosa's eyes are wide, searching for something in Rafael's eyes.

"Rafael, tell him to stay. Don't take him away from me."

Rafael ignores her pleas. For once he wanted to be selfish.

Rosa tries to restrain the child, but he breaks away from her and goes with his father. Why the determination to go with his father? There was a lot of homemade food at home and he wanted to eat it.

Rafael tries to persuade the five-year-old boy to stay with his mother, but the child is quite stubborn, so he chooses to give in. Rosa hugs both of them goodbye.

The little boy's name is Geronimo Ayala.

When they arrived back into their home, Rafael acted differently. His behavior could be described as love sick, but it can be most accurately described as depressed. The loneliness and sadness were a heavy burden on Rafael. He found himself in a circle that seemed impossible to step out of. Rafael would tell his son that he was the sole reason why he still pushed through life. Time passed and Geronimo still waited for his mother and sibling to arrive. He came to miss them quite significantly, and frequently asked his father when they would be arriving. Don Chema, the landowner took care of him while his father went out to work, but Geronimo could not help but feel lonely.

Don Chema insisted on helping Rafael. He could sense the sadness that was eating him alive. Chema suggests that he travel back to his wife and bring her and the kids back. Eventually Don Chema's stubborn promptings did help Rafael make his mind up. Soon enough Rafael was off to bring his wife and children back.

Geronimo never saw his father, mother, or siblings ever again.

The sun is still high up on the sky, but his stomach is calling out to him. As per usual he makes his way towards the kitchen. He finds himself following a smell. He is intrigued as to why the smell is familiar to him. Tears start spilling as he spots a figure's backside; something tells him it is his mother. Suddenly the figure turns around. It is her, but she does not look how he remembers her. Age has arrived to her body, her hair is completely grey and her face has wrinkles around her eyes. She does not speak, but she does extend her hands to reach his face. He starts to become smaller, and his mother starts looking young again. He is fully embraced by her. Sorrow, loss, and memories flood back into his mind as he sits in his bed.

This is not the first time such dreams have come to Geronimo. They always left him with a sour taste of the past. He threw himself on his work on those days, hoping to forget all about the incident. He would rather not think of the past, saddened by the thought that both of his parents had abandoned him. On those days he chose not to say much, and was easily angered. Both actions were normal for him; no one ever noticed that there was something different about his daily thoughts. Geronimo was not the kind of man to openly express his feelings. This day was different. Instead of feeling anger and resentment he felt melancholic sitting on his bed. He peered outside. The sun was greeting the sleepy surroundings.

When Geronimo was storing food, the thoughts came back. This time they were different. *Mami. I miss her. What does she look like now? Is she still as beautiful?* Carlos, one of Geronimo's sons had noticed his father's tears. He knew better than to ask him what was wrong. Who knows what card he would pull out? *Que muchachito tan metiche.* He did not want to be called nosy again. He wondered what was making his father, one of the toughest men he knew, weep like a child. Then his father suddenly stopped crying, he wiped his tears and he looked around. Carlos quickly hid; he did not want to be caught by his father. Geronimo was so entranced in his thoughts that when he passed a shaking Carlos he did not even notice him. He decided to make a trip to El Salvador to look for his mother.

Geronimo had a habit of departing on trips at random times; it drew his wife crazy when they first married. Juana never quite knew when she would become a widow. She turned to religion to have some sense of purpose besides looking after their children. She liked to believe she had some control over her husband's extended rendezvous to who knows where. Geronimo packed a few of his belongings and walked out of his house, then out of the village entirely. He did not tell anyone where he is going, he just told his partner that he would be out for a while.

La Montañita is located in the Northern region of Honduras. It is closer to Guatemala than El Salvador. Geronimo had always known his mother was a citizen of El Salvador, therefore his destination was determined. There were several flaws in his plan. He had no direct destination in mind, therefore he would have to ask around and hopefully find someone who recognized his mother name. It was like shooting a single light ray into an abyss of sleeping beasts, since tensions between Honduras and El Salvador were not the best in those days. Although the 100 Hours War, also known as the Football War, had occurred in 1969, tensions between the borders were still quite tedious.

Rosa Ayala was a name that cannot disappear from Geronimo's mind. *Where has this woman been hiding? Why did she never come back for her eldest?* Geronimo could not help but feel hurt every time he had to utter her name. *What has she been up to all this time? What will I face when I arrive? What about my siblings, did they never feel curious about their elder brother? Did they deem me dead in their minds?* Geronimo's growing concern eventually overpowered his ego. His ego, in fact, was the only factor that had been holding him from looking into his mother and siblings through the decades. With his ego in his stomach, Geronimo asked around about the Ayala family. Eventually he landed a village.

Geronimo arrived at his destination. He spotted the elderly woman sitting in a rocking chair in front of the house. Her eyes sparked with recognition of the seeming stranger. She s clueless as to why she had a strong desire to weep, as tears slightly started to blur her sight. Geronimo felt his heart racing; could the woman sitting be his mother? Geronimo introduced himself.

"Hello, I am looking for a Rosa Ayala. My name is Geronimo Ayala, her son."

The woman looked alert for a moment, her suspicions were proven correctly; it was him. Anna had dreamed this moment many times, but she had never figured it would actually happen now. She sighed and swallowed her tears, however her voice trembled when started to speak.

"My name is Anna Ayala, Rosa's sister." She rubbed her eyes; she had forgotten how Rosa's children looked. Out of all the children Rosa and Rafael had, their eldest was the only one who balanced out his mother's and father's drastic looks. He had his father's dark complexion, his eyes, and tall height. But his mouth, nose, and smile were just like his mother's. They hugged, and she couldn't help but blurt out that he had his father's mischievous eyes. Anna was a woman who was relatively short in stature, her hair was completely grey and there was this amorous aura to her. He smiled tenderly at her.

"You are quite handsome. Did you know that?"

"Maybe," he responded out of habit. They both started laughing. Anna tapped Geronimo's shoulder as she spoke to him, turning to sit back in her seat again.

"Geronimo, I suggest you sit next to me, *mijo*. You are not going to like the news." Anna patted the seat next to her. They sat together in silence for a brief moment, Anna was thinking of a way she could deliver the news to him.

"She is no longer alive is she?" Geronimo may be a campesino, but he was no *bruto*.

Anna let out a long sigh and nodded her head. "You know your father visited after they decided to separate…"

It was in winter time when Rafael went to try and meet his beloved Rosa. Winter time in Central America is brutal. Yes, there is no snow and no real cold. But lord do the skies know how to weep, and not only for hours, but days on end. Still, Rafael fought the horrible weather. He did feel guilty that he left his son with someone else, but it was not like Don Chema was a stranger. As the train glided across the railroad tracks, Rafael's mind couldn't help but naturally drift to Rosa. He could envision her next to him this very moment. Her blue eyes would search the sky and her soft yellow hair would blow in the wind. Her mouth would whisper something about the cold weather, and she would shiver and huddle close to him while he chuckled. Her cheeks and nose would be slightly reddened because of the chilly wind. He missed her so much.

The pueblo looked different in the weather; it looked uninhabited, which is odd for a city that always seemed to be bustling back in the days when Rosa and Rafael were youthful. A ghost town where the only sounds that seemed to come out through the tightly closed doors were those of sheer horror. When Rafael arrived at the Ayala's household his fear materialized to realization. When Rosa and Rafael agreed to part, he would have never imagined that they would see each other, yet he found himself staring at her from a distance. Rosa looked very different this time; the color seemed to have washed out of her system. As Rafael approached her he followed her gaze, which fell upon one of their children.

"Papi al fin veniste?" the child asked. The others lifted their heads from their pillows.

"It is daddy!" Rafael gave them a weak smile and gave all of them a kiss on the forehead.

"Alright children, your father and I need to speak outside." As soon as they stepped a foot outside the room, Rafael could not help but start crying; all of their babies looked half alive.

"You should have told me, Rosa."

Rosa only moved her head. She had developed bags under her eyes. She looked really skinny too.

"They will get better, right?"

Rosa looked at him dead in the eye, and shook her head no.

"You have been drained of tears, haven't you?"

She nodded.

Time passed, and eventually the children started to not wake up. Rosa fell into such a hole that after all of them were not breathing, she became bedridden. Eventually, her heart stopped beating as well. Rafael buried her and left the town. There wasn't a day after Rosa's death that Rafael was sober. Yet he decided that it was finally time to return to Geronimo. He was the only family left for the child; however, things did not end how he wanted it to end. Rafael did not survive the trip.

Geronimo now understood that his mother had not abandoned him, but that she was busy rescuing his siblings. Geronimo bid everyone in the house farewell, and he headed home.

Geronimo Ayala was my grandfather. For all of his life, even at an older age, he was notorious for disappearing without a word and reappearing later on as if nothing had happened. Every time he walked out into the distance, no one knew when he would return. One fateful day my grandfather took a trip that he never could return home from. Soon it will be the seventh anniversary of his death.

Elizabeth

Mexico

I am Mexican-American. My parents were both born in Mexico, and I was born in the U.S. However, I wasn't raised here. My mom moved to Mexico very shortly after giving birth to live back with her mom, siblings, and the rest of her family as she had fallen into depression.

Mexico is known for a lot of things. The food, the music, the clothing, yet this chapter is about neither of those things. Mexico is also known for its legends, and for its witchcraft. As crazy as it sounds, witchcraft is believed to have originated in the small city of Veracruz. Coincidentally, this is the city in which I grew up in.

Many people are skeptical about demons, ghosts, curses and a lot of other similar concepts. This chapter will definitely change anyone's mind.

My sister and I were very young after we moved to Mexico. We didn't do much but run around playing with my grandma's animals. Yet, life was happening all around us. The first story my mom told us about her temporary trip back to Mexico with us was a story about her aunt.

My mom had an aunt who was a very scary woman. She was small, under five feet tall but with the meanest face possible. There were many rumors swarming around town about her and the things that went on in her house behind closed doors.

My mom often took my sister and I out to various places so that we could see as much about Mexico as possible. My favorite was the river that was right in my grandma's backyard. The water was clear, and it was only about two feet deep. I loved to go "swimming" (I can't swim. Not even to this day) at night, as my grandma's porch lights casted an orange glow over the water. One night, my sister and I were wrapping ourselves in towels after getting out of the water. We headed inside, and my mom decided to stay out a little longer. Eventually, my grandma tucked us into bed.

As my mom sat alone, she dozed off into a light sleep. It was a warm night, with a cool breeze. A loud splash coming from the river woke my mom up. She looked up, and with her perfect 20/20 vision was able to make out her small aunt several feet to the left of her. Her aunt was standing in the water. Just standing. My mom continued to watch her. After a couple minutes, her aunt finally moved. She plunged herself deeper into the water, starting with her legs. She bent her knees until she was on the floor. She was almost entirely underwater, and in a few seconds laid all the way down. My mom stared. She was frozen, and wasn't sure what to do.

The first question that came to her head was "Did my aunt just commit suicide right in front of me?" but she quickly dismissed this thought as she saw her aunt's arms and legs moving slightly. My mom continued to stare at her aunt laying underwater. After about an hour or two, she began to doze off once again. This time, she woke up within minutes as she heard another loud splash.

It was her aunt, who was finally stepping out of the water in the shape of a pig. A very big pig. Yes, a pig.

My mom's aunt was a shapeshifter. And that was the first sign of the crazy reality of my Mexican family.

Following the rest of my short childhood in Mexico, strange things did certainly continue to happen, mostly around the house. My grandma had a painting of her dad, my great grandpa, hanging in her living room. It might sound cliché, but his eyes would follow my sister, my mom and I around the living room. My grandma had a priest come in and "clean our house," where he politely asked my great grandpa to leave because he was scaring us. Later that night, my mom dreamt of her grandfather.

"He apologized," she told us the next morning. "He said he was sorry for scaring us, he just wanted to see his girls."

He never came back after that day.

As I grew up, I did not continue my childhood in Mexico. My mom moved back to the U.S. in time for my sister and I to start kindergarten. Yet the weird stuff never really stopped.

When my mom, sister and I returned to the United States I decided I was fascinated with the stories I would hear about Mexico over dinner. My mom began to visit my grandpa a lot more, as he was older and knew of more stories to share with me. He considered himself a *brujo*, a man with the ability to do witchcraft to help people in sickness. I loved going to his house to hear his stories. When I was around 8 years old, my grandpa finally opened up about all the times he used his abilities in a dark way. Helping those in sickness is not the only way a *brujo* can work his magic. Their special abilities are also able to grant harm to others around them, or to deal with paranormal activity.

The first "scary" story my grandpa ever told me was about a poor woman who lived close to his hometown back in Mexico. Her firstborn son had a tendency to lock himself in the darkest room of their house: the closet. Pressing her ear against the door, the woman would hear her son whispering, followed by laughing fits. When she finally asked him who he was talking to, he replied with, "Me. He's me. He has the same name as me and he looks just like me. He's my friend."

The woman became terrified. She immediately contacted my grandpa with the story, begging for help. Unfortunately, she had nothing to give to him in return. My grandpa being the kind man that he is helped the woman. He gave her a procedure written on a piece of paper. It required plants and a pair of scissors to be placed under the boy's pillow as he slept. Sure enough, the little boy never walked into the closet again.

When I first heard this story, I tried to envision the terrified mother and her happy little son. I wasn't sure what to picture them like. I also tried to give life to their little house, and the dark closet in my head. Eventually, the story drifted from my mind until a few years later.

I was 13 when I had the dream.

I was in my house, sitting on my bottom bunk of the bed. I was listening to a tiny voice coming from my closed closet door. After a few minutes, I finally got up and slowly opened the door. I wasn't scared.

Inside was a little boy sitting in the dark. His little legs were crossed, and his eyes were staring straight ahead at what is very hard to describe. It was him, the same two little boys staring at each other. They were identical, as if there was a mirror placed in between them.

There wasn't.

One of the boys turned to face me. He was a beautiful toddler. His smile was big, with perfect cheekbones at each end. The other followed a few seconds later. They both laughed.

"You opened the door!" the one on the right yelled in glee.

He got up and began to run around my room. The second toddler stayed on the closet floor. I stared at the toddler who was still sitting. His smile was a little more shy, but soon enough he too got up to run.

I talked to my grandpa about my dream. I asked him to describe to me the little boy he had visited years before. I had a strong feeling that that was the boy in my dream.

"He was a toddler. He was adorable and full of life. His smile was shy at first, but he warmed up to me in a matter of minutes, and continued to play around his house. His dark hair matched his dark eyes perfectly."

I sat in fascination. It was him! I was right! I saw him in my dream. You would think I was terrified, right? No. I was amazed.

The more stories my grandpa told me, the more visions I began to have in my dreams. I envisioned the people and the places in my sleep. Since the age of 13, I had some of the worst nightmares. Some of the stories my grandpa would tell were truly terrifying. There were times in which my dreams would change. They'd be influenced from what I'd hear during the day, but would have their own spin to them. Shortly, my sister started to complain about my sleeping habits. We've always shared a room, and she began to hear me in my sleep. She would tell me the next morning that I was crying in my sleep the night before. I would also moan and softly call for help. It terrified her.

As I grew older, the dreams (more like nightmares) came to a halt when I was 16 years old. They didn't start back up until half a year later, when I was 17 and a half years old.

This next part is going to sound very unreal. But, I promise everything is true.

I have a habit of showering very late. After I get home from school, I usually arrive to eat an early dinner and watch a little bit of Netflix in the meantime. Following that, I start any homework I can before working at the clinic. I usually get home from work at 10 pm, and by then I'm a little hungry again, so I have a somewhat heavy snack while I finish the homework I started. Usually around midnight, I am ready to shower to be ready for bed.

Sometimes it happens while I'm in the shower, but it's usually after I'm already out. While I'm getting dressed, I hear my mom's voice calling my name so close to the door, I imagine she's pressing her face against the wood. Yet, my mom is asleep. She is not at the door. In all honesty, it terrifies me. I can feel the color draining from my face, and I can feel my blood get cold whenever I hear my mom's voice, knowing she is asleep. Other times, there would be constant knocking on the door. Sometimes just 2 or 3 in a row, soft knocks. Other times it'd be a really loud one that almost shakes the door.

As I already mentioned, I was still having really bad nightmares. I would also have frequent lucid dreams. Those were never really scary, though. They were actually kind of realistic. The most memorable one was a nurse who had visited me. She stood at the foot of my bed and asked me if I was doing okay. I was. She came closer after every question, yet all I had to do was not look her directly in the eyes. Then she was gone.

Over the summer of 2018 I began to see people in my dreams. I know, it sounds pretty dumb. But it's true. It started off with two children. In those dreams, I'd be sitting at my vanity, carefully applying makeup onto my face using the mirror. Now, I have horrible eyesight. I have to literally press almost my entire face to the mirror. Looking closely at my face, I saw the two kids in the mirror. A boy and a girl. It was so cliché. They were dressed as if they came from another time period. The girl's hair was in two pigtails, and I can't remember what the little boy's hair looked like. The second person was a man. I would dream about watching TV in the living room and while I watched, he watched me. He also looked like he was from a different time period. He was wearing overalls over a long sleeve t-shirt, and for some reason I also can't remember what his hair looked like.

Maybe it was my imagination, but I started to see them outside of my dreams, too. In the exact same places that they appeared at in my sleep. Whenever I was getting ready, the kids appeared behind me, and whenever I would watch TV alone, the man would appear beside me. It wasn't until after a few weeks that they vanished. I don't remember them very clearly anymore.

As of now, I don't have dreams about stories my grandpa would tell me anymore. The kids and the man are gone too. I stopped showering when everyone else was asleep too, just in case. Every now and then I get an uneasy feeling or hear something strange. I try my best to ignore it though. I still get pretty bad nightmares, and I still cry in my sleep.

I talked to my closest friend about all my crazy visions and dreams, and he advised me to place a bible under my pillow while I slept. I considered it in the moment, but then realized it might actually have no effect. I don't believe in the Bible. I'm not sure about God, but definitely not the Bible. If anything, it might've even given me more nightmares. One thing's for certain though: I am terrified of the dark.

Esli

Honduras

I believe there is nothing wrong with feeling pride with the nation you were born in. Sure, everyone has their criticisms of what could be improved on, but there is always a reassurance when individuals have a conclusive location in which they could call "home." Home has always been the location in which my nuclear family has decided to temporarily live in. But soon enough I will become an adult-in-the-making, meaning that I will have to redefine what my idea of home is.

My citizenship is legally from Honduras, since I was born there. But I find it extremely difficult to proudly regard myself as a Honduran due to my lack of knowledge on anything regarding the country besides very basic facts. I was primarily raised in the United States, I am basically an American, but I am not at the same time. I, of course, lack the papers to prove my American-ness. But more importantly I lack the enthusiasm to become a documented United States citizen.

Sure, the benefits are nice. I would like to learn how to drive without having to worry that a cop will deport me to the country I know zero about. And yes, I would like to not worry about getting sick because if my sickness becomes serious it would lead to my parents falling into a huge amount of debt that they would not be able to pay with the low wages they currently receive. Because yes, the healthcare system is ridiculously overpriced in America, and they definitely do take advantage of those who do not have proper documentation. And of course I would love to not have the higher education system literally be against my legal existence. If it's hard for the average student in America, imagine being a not-so-smart illegal alien who has no real talent nor persevering passion towards anything. Trying to sell yourself as a good student to the colleges so they could give you more money when the only thing you are really good at is working hard, needless to say raises eyebrows.

But what does it mean to be an American when you do not gain citizenship through your birth? To me it means I would have to build my life up from scratch, more specifically my social association with my parents. I can't see myself trying to become a citizen; it would feel like a betrayal to my parents. The thought sounds extremely silly but it's a concern I hold. Not that my parents would mind if I change my citizenship; they see me as more of an American than a Honduran anyway, but there is a fear that strikes my heart that since I did not experience Honduras that I might make the wrong decision by changing my citizenship. I know that the Honduras they speak about is long gone, but what if what I seek for is in Honduras? Can I really find happiness in a country that is falling into shambles? All I hear about the country is that it is heavy with crime, poverty, and corrupted politicians. But is that representative of the country as a whole?

At times I just wish I could not have citizenship from any country, and no longer be associated with any sort of politics. I want to be able to find someplace, something, or heck even someone to make me feel at home. That someone or even a group of people does not even have to be a romantic partner, just people who I could cherish and appreciate to have in my life. My hope is that I will finally feel more at home when I stop closing myself off to people. That I should give them a chance, and maybe *just maybe* finally feel at home in an oppressive country.

Maybe yearning for someone as a home feels like a stretch. Will I ever be able to open up to someone? Could they fully open up to me? Can we talk about the significant events yet giggle about very immature small events? A person who can not only lend a shoulder but also offer advice? Talk about anything while doing nothing? Respect each other's different views and not make the other feel uncomfortable when opinions differentiate? Can I find someone who I could just hang out with and not feel the need to constantly talk to? Can I find someone or a group of people who I could just hang out and finish work with? Just me and someone else in the same space? Someone who I can speak to about more than just school?

What is home? Location wise you could say it is Durham. Although I know much of the history of Durham and despite the fact that I have lived in the city for about a decade, I have yet to venture out with friends and explore. Speaking of Durham, the city has drastically changed and specifically towards the Hispanic/Latinx community. Yes, Durham is no

Miami, but in a country that is supposed to be big and oppressive, Durham feels warm and welcoming. I know many of my peers want to escape Durham as soon as they graduate, but I have no such innate feeling. Maybe I don't see it in that light because I rarely venture out anyways.

I remember sitting at a "Baby R Us" location talking to an adult and "translating" for my parents. At the time Durham had a huge Hispanic/Latinx community but the area had yet to hire bilingual staff to help around the community. I was nine years old at the time, and I could see my parents visibly frustrated because I was not translating in a coherent manner. I would just repeat the English words with a Spanish accent; it's bilingual culture – I used to say a Spanish word in an English accent when I was learning English. It was during these times that my mom had not taken her Durham Tech English classes. I remember not wanting to leave home in those days. Anywhere we went I would be used as a translator, and my parents would express frustration.

It is not like that anymore; times have changed. My mom can understand and communicate with others in English – partly due to her job and because of the classes she religiously took at Durham Tech. I can say a phrase to my mother without having an itching feeling in my throat to try and translate so she could understand what I am saying. Durham itself has also changed. There are more Latinx establishments, and big corporations having more bilingual people on deck is very helpful to my parents.

My father, on the other hand, is still adamant about not learning English. "What good will it do, *mija*?" he says. I admit it becomes frustrating at times to properly communicate with my father, and sometimes I am painfully reminded that he received a limited education, both in English and Spanish. Sometimes my father arrives home from his job as a dishwasher and asks me what a word means. I see the hurt and frustration in his eyes as he tries to make sense of the strange word. Every time he brings such words home, he brings a story to go along with what happened at work. The story normally involves waiters and their foolish tantrums; my father tends to misinterpret their behavior to be directed to him. What he doesn't know is that he is the most respected person in the kitchen. You will not find my father complaining, badmouthing, or even disrespecting a person. In fact, he always does his best to keep a smile in a world where he barely understands the language.

You may be wondering why it is that I am mentioning my family in a piece that is centered around what home is to me. That is a question that I find myself frequently asking as I am writing this. Maybe family is not just my nuclear family; it is the language, my mother's cooking, and the comfort that I will not be judged for being myself. Can I make anywhere my home if I find a place where I feel comfortable to be myself? Should I call my home the members of my high school class? Can I consider the counselors that have given me confidence, voice, and assurance as home?

My high school is not a location that I would consider home, but in a way it kind of is. I feel comfort that I know the school's schedule and hallways. Everyone is gathered at lunch around a specific time, and everyone is heading to their class on time. Maybe home is the comfort I feel when I fall into a routine.

Language is also important on the concept of home. I speak Spanish at home, and English almost anywhere else. I subconsciously change my language when talking to my parents, and refer to Spanish when in a Latinx establishment. My Spanish is very informal. I probably have the select vocabulary of a twelve-year-old. I tend to switch many things up; in English everything is in reverse – instead of *casa blanca* which directly translates to "house white," proper English would be "white house." My parents are used to constantly correcting my speech. I will say that at times I am discouraged to share my stories because of the overwhelming shame I feel that I cannot speak the language that is primarily used in Honduras.

On the topic of language I recently discovered some interesting facts about Honduras. In Latin countries certain dances are associated with countries, and *punta* is associated with Honduras. *Punta* is a dance and music spoken in Garifuna, which is a language that is often associated with Garinagu (an ethnic group that is of African descent) population in Honduras. Honduras is known to be ninety percent *mestizos*, which is a common term used to refer to people of Spanish and indigenous descent. For example, I would be considered a *mestiza*.

Back in the 90's, *punta* started garnering much attention, however one was not seeing many Garinagu on TV; instead one saw *mestizos* singing and performing music. Granted the lyrics could be from Garifuna, Kriol, English, or Spanish. Garifuna and Spanish tend to be most popular in Honduras. However, most songs tend to be in indigenous Arawak, which I may add is the language of indigenous people of South America and the Caribbean. Why did I just suddenly throw all that information on you? I will admit I did not know this information until I remembered that I have heard *punta* sung in a language that I did not recognize. It is moments like this that I am proud of being a descendant from such a culturally rich country.

I like to think I am a person who is looking for a home, but as I kept thinking I could not help but think that I may already have one. They say home is where one feels comfort, and I feel comfortable standing in the "no man's land."

Ezra

Kenya

Africa
The neglected continent,
The poor continent
Filled with black people,
Filled with misery
That's my continent,
And that's how people view it
But let me tell you about the real Africa,
My home
A land filled with love,
A land where no one judges you
About your color, your identity, or anything
A place where you feel safe
Filled with water all around us,
Filled with love in all hearts,
Filled with knowledge in all minds,
That's my continent

A place where your neighbor is your friend,
Where your neighbor feeds you,
Where your neighbor isn't just a neighbor
He/She is your friend, your family
A place you are proud to call home,
Where differences are celebrated,
That's my home,
That's Africa
No matter how people try to decimate her,
How many problems she has faced,
She never loses her focus,
To fight for her children
So forget what other people say about her,
Go and try to see it for yourself,
You'll find there is no place like Africa,
She takes care of her own.
I end with this,
Don't try to tarnish our image,
Because we will only rise stronger,
Because that's what we do,
That is Africa.

I was born in a country called the Democratic Republic of Congo. We moved to Kenya when I was nine years old. I have one sister and I'm the only son, also the first born in our family. An adventure awaited us in Kenya.

Kenya is one of the most developed counties in Africa, so when we went there it was like we had entered in another continent. Aside from being developed, it was very challenging to anyone who has never been to Kenya, especially me and my family. I went with my mother, my sister and some of my cousins, so it was really nice and fun.

The first day I went to school I was so happy until they told me that the national languages of Kenya were English and Swahili. I was shocked beyond anything because I didn't know either of those languages. So I asked if I could go home. When I reached home my mom was not there, so I just sat there until she came home from work. She knew Swahili so it wasn't hard for her to find a job. When she entered into the house, she came into my room because the principal had told her what happened. She sat there with me for hours. When it was time to eat supper, she told me to come and go eat. After the meal we had our fun conversations with the whole family (it is kind of our thing) and they told me to go back to school, work hard and show them that I can do it.

I went to school the next day and the teachers told me that they are going to help me but it won't be easy; one, there are beatings (not like fighting or throwing punches). They said it was to help me, so I agreed because it happens in Kenya to all the students. I went to class and the teacher introduced me; at break time there were some boys who came to see me and we became friends, especially the ones in my class. Even though I did not understand what they were saying, I still liked them.

As days went by I began to learn English and Swahili slowly, because of my friends and watching TV, and mostly because of my English teacher. He would give me this creepy skull every time I spoke Swahili instead of English, and I had to keep the skull for the whole day hanging around my neck. To me that was the thing that helped me a lot, and I will always be thankful to that teacher for what he did, so that I could learn and understand English.

The other things I loved about being at school were the games. We had school championships, and that to me was very fun because I love playing soccer and I was accepted to play for the school team. I was so happy to play my first game. Even though we lost, it was still a huge and happy moment for me that will always remain in my head.

The next year before I came to school, I practiced English and Swahili throughout the whole holiday we were home. When my English teacher saw me he wanted to know if I had improved, so he called me to the office. He asked me to explain to him everything that I did throughout the holiday. I asked him if I could write it in an essay but he refused, saying I might get some help from my friends. I had no other choice, so I told him everything in English, and he was so happy, along with the other teachers. The face he had after my story, it's still stuck in my head to this day.

Kenya may not be the country that I was born in, but I am very glad I got to experience the thrill it gave me, and I would not exchange it for another. Kenya is a good country filled with a lot of hardships, not only to immigrants coming in, but also to its people. So whenever my mood would go down, Kenya had this way of entertaining people like going to concerts or going to watch soccer games, where I met my first coach. He is one of the people who helped with my soccer career and also made sure I was doing well in school. He basically became like my uncle. He would give me advice on how to live not only in school but also how to live outside, along with my teachers who made sure I got used to living in a brand new country without speaking the language, yet they took their time to make sure I would not give up my studies because they understood the importance of studying. The people who inspired me were my family and mostly my coach, because he was from here in the U.S., he told me to be able to live here I had to study hard especially since my mother did not know English and we were not coming here with my father, so I put in all my effort and eventually it paid off. I am very thankful for all who encouraged me and to those who are still doing it.

Kathya

Mexico

I am both a Mexican and an American citizen. As a Latina, I think it's almost mandatory for me to talk about the stereotypes that people spread, and growing up in a country where I don't look like I belong.

I am lucky to say that I was never bullied at school growing up. My skin is tan, and I have frizzy curly hair, yet no one ever teased me about the way I look. I'm not saying racial bullying isn't a thing, but I also cannot say I have experienced it. The main difference between my friends and I as we grew up wasn't our physical appearances. It was my parent's immigration status.

First off, I cannot stress enough how hard life is for an immigrant. Could you imagine leaving your country to come to a bigger one, with more advanced technology in every way possible? Could you imagine hearing and seeing strange words everywhere you go? I definitely can't.

Growing up, immediately after I learned some basic English in preschool, I became my mom's personal interpreter. I had barely mastered the English language, and she was already using me EVERYWHERE. To order Whoppers, coffee, or to pay the rent at the main office of our apartment complex. I was all over the place. Of course I didn't mind. I was glad to help. It felt like such an important role: helping my mother understand a language she didn't speak. And I started as early as the age of four.

As my mom was raising my sister and I, she worked three jobs. She was a waitress at a small Mexican restaurant, a cook at Pizza Hut, and a cashier at a Mexican store. All of these jobs were minimum wage. It was the best she could find, though, considering her circumstances. There were a couple days a week in which she couldn't handle my sister and I, therefore we stayed at my grandpa's house. He was our babysitter. We spend a lot of time with my grandpa, (my dad's dad) eventually resulting in us growing a very strong bond. We became inseparable, the three of us.

Unfortunately, when I was 14 years old my grandpa got into a pretty bad accident. He required a lawyer and everything. It was kind of like something from a movie. He was okay, though. Because of the accident my grandpa was able to become an American resident, also known as acquiring a "green card." With his green card, he was granted a license and a work permit. He got a job at a factory, and he bought a new car with his savings. He was living his best life.

The thing about green cards is that they can sometimes be really complicated. There are different kinds, and different ways to obtain one. It's kind of hard to explain the many ways in which a green card works. My grandpa didn't fully understand either. He met up regularly with his lawyer just to make sure things were going smoothly. A decent paying job and a license? It sounded a little too good to be true. And it was.

My grandpa got deported on the way to the office in Raleigh. Now, it's not very clear why he did. Before getting his green card, my grandpa had gotten in trouble with the law, as the result of driving without a license even after being caught. It happens more often than anyone would think. ICE tracks down immigrants even after innocence, or a minor crime. That's where they get you.

My grandpa was locked up for a few months until he was finally shipped to his home city in Oaxaca, Mexico. Mexico is very different than the U.S. Mexicans don't hire elderly people. The elderly have to figure it out for themselves. My grandma has to send my grandpa money at least every two weeks. Every month, she sends a box full of toiletries such as deodorant, toothpaste, floss, and other little trinkets such as gloves for the winter time, a mini umbrella for rain. A few candy bars. The closest store to my grandpa's little hometown is almost an hour away. He doesn't have a car, and transportation is too scary for him considering his age.

My grandma is a cook at Pizza Hut. She makes $9.50 an hour, and with that she has to provide for herself and for her husband in a whole different country.

So what was that racist stereotype? Mexicans are taking American jobs? If immigrants who speak no English whatsoever, who are completely foreign to the United States are taking jobs, I guess that you need to work a little harder.